Learning
from
Children

Alan R. Sadovnik and Susan F. Semel
General Editors

Vol. 38

PETER LANG
New York • Washington, D.C./Baltimore • Bern
Frankfurt am Main • Berlin • Brussels • Vienna • Oxford

Mary E. Hauser

Learning
from
Children

The Life and Legacy
of Caroline Pratt

PETER LANG
New York • Washington, D.C./Baltimore • Bern
Frankfurt am Main • Berlin • Brussels • Vienna • Oxford

Library of Congress Cataloging-in-Publication Data

Hauser, Mary E.
Learning from children: the life and legacy of Caroline Pratt / Mary Hauser.
p. cm. — (History of schools and schooling; vol. 38)
Includes bibliographical references and index.
1. Pratt, Caroline, b. 1867. 2. Women educators—New York—Biography. I. Title.
LA2317.P72H38   370.92—dc22 [B]   2006018960
ISBN 0-8204-6751-0
ISSN 1089-0678

Bibliographic information published by **Die Deutsche Bibliothek**.
Die Deutsche Bibliothek lists this publication in the "Deutsche
Nationalbibliografie"; detailed bibliographic data is available
on the Internet at http://dnb.ddb.de/.

Cover design by Joni Holst
Cover photographs courtesy of the City and Country School Archives,
New York, New York.

© 2006 Peter Lang Publishing, Inc., New York
29 Broadway, New York, NY 10006
www.peterlang.com

Printed in the United States of America

For

Katie Quinn Randall

and

Charles Carter Randall

I am very proud to be your Grandma Mary.
I wish for you the kind of educational experience
that Caroline Pratt envisioned for all children.

Contents

Illustrations

Acknowledgments

I deeply appreciate the enthusiastic assistance I received from the following individuals and institutions:

City and Country School Archives, Wendy Bouthillier, Director of Development, for extensive use of the archives and permission to reproduce photographs of Caroline Pratt and of the classrooms.

Fayetteville Free Library, Fayetteville, New York, Linda M. Ryan, Assistant Director.

Library of Congress, Manuscript Division, Washington D.C.

Milbank Memorial Library, Special Collections, Teachers College, Columbia University, David Ment and Hal B. Grossman.

Manlius New York Town Historian, Barbara Rivette, for informative correspondence and for sharing a photo of Lizzie Pratt, Caroline's sister.

Sam Stack, University of West Virginia, for sharing Elsie Ripley Clapp archival material.

Associates of the City and Country School for their perspectives
Orlen Donaldson	Margery Franklin
Sally Cartwright	Sylvia Miller
Harriet Cuffaro	Virginia Parker

Scott Johnston, Osaka Jyogakuin College, Japan, for extensive critical reading.

I owe a very special acknowledgment to Series Editors Alan Sadovnik and Susan Semel for their confidence in my ability to produce this biography and for permission to use material I previously published in their edited volume, *Founding Mothers and Others: Women Educational Leaders During the Progressive Era.*

Friends and family have had more to do with the preparation of Caroline Pratt's story than they probably wanted to at times. Their support and encouragement and friendly reading have been greatly appreciated. As I write their names, I realize that they may be more pleased than I am about the completion of this book. Now they may be able to talk with me about other topics, and ask questions other than "How is the book coming?"

I wish to offer thanks to: family members—my brother John Fink, my sister-in-law Joy Hauser, parents of my wonderful grandchildren, Debra and Charles Randall; my niece, Cynthia Carlson, and friends— (listed alphabetically) Jan Jipson, Margot Kennard, Shirley Kessler, Marilyn Meyer, Michele Neidich, Nancy Scherr, John Siebold, Lois and Bill Tetzlaff. Margie Geasler and Jim Achterberg as well as Sandy Theunick and Dennis Fisher welcomed me to their guest rooms during my research travels.

The most important thank you goes to Jerry Randall. The nature of our unique relationship defies any descriptors I can think of using!

Abbreviations

CCSA	City and Country School Archives, New York
CP	Caroline Pratt
CU	Columbia University Rare Book and Manuscript Library
FFL	Fayetteville Free Library, Fayetteville, New York
ILFC	*I Learn from Children*, Caroline Pratt, 1970 New York: Harper & Row [1948 N.Y. Simon & Schuster]
LC	Library of Congress Manuscript Division, Washington, D.C., LaFollette Family Collection
MML	Milbank Memorial Library, Teachers College, Columbia University, New York

Figure 1. Caroline Pratt in her office.

Prologue

Do you remember being in kindergarten?

In kindergarten, you probably spent time in the block corner, building with a set of smooth unpainted blocks, the kind that had squares that were half the size of rectangles, and cylinders that were just as tall as the rectangles. You probably took field trips—maybe to the post office or the fire station or the farm. Chances are that your memories of these kindergarten activities might be some of the best of your whole school life. Chances are that you never thought about where they originated. Kindergarten was just kindergarten, it just happened. But there is a story behind unit blocks and field trips.

These nearly universal kindergarten experiences are examples of Caroline Pratt's legacy to children. She devised and made the first set of those wonderful unit blocks for a school she founded in New York City in 1914. She was an early advocate of the value of learning outside of the classroom. She regularly took her students on field trips in order to have direct experiences with the world around them. She recognized the ability of young children to construct their knowledge about the world and created a unique classroom environment for their use. She had many innovative ideas about the teaching and learning process that she put into practice in her school, ideas that can inspire and renew educators as we try to maintain our ideals in a time when education at all levels is under intense scrutiny to be accountable in ways that good educators know do not help children to be successful.

Imagine a school organized around the principle that a school should nourish rather than stifle students' natural curiosity. Visualize students doing "real" work—operating a school store, providing postal services, designing and producing signage for the school—in the context of learning reading and mathematics. Picture art, music, and movement as integral parts of students' experience. This biography celebrates the life and work of the woman who made such a learning environment a reality. How and where she got her ideas and put them into practice is a story I want to tell—to pay tribute to an educator who can inspire all of us who are advocates for the children we teach.

CHAPTER ONE

Introduction

*Curiosity, that life-giving human attribute,
is nourished only by discovery.
To discover is to live at the highest pitch
of interest and concentration*[1]

CAROLINE PRATT WROTE THOSE WORDS about her educational philosophy; however, they also apply to the life she led. She had a personal lifelong curiosity about how children learn and a professional desire to create environments to stimulate the curiosity and learning of children. Her personal (private) and professional (public) lives were both shaped by discovery through direct experience and observation. So all encompassing was her passion for her work with children that it is difficult to discern the boundaries between her public and private selves. But it is the totality of her work and life that is important, because it represents part of a legacy that can illuminate our thinking about children and our work with them. Through Caroline Pratt's story, the past can speak to the future. Her work can give clarity to the issues we struggle with as we attempt to meet children's needs in a society characterized by social change as dramatic today as it was during the progressive era when she was developing her education practices.

Who was this woman who contributed so much to educational thought and practice and about whom we know so little? Caroline Louise Pratt was born in Fayetteville, New York, in 1867. She died in New York City in 1954. Those facts are bookends for the volumes of knowledge that the life lived between those dates have to offer educators. Caroline Pratt's story can inspire as well as challenge modern readers. Her life and her work can inform the life and work of those of us who toil in the field of education, as advocates for children, as feminists, and as educational reformers who seek progressive teaching practices for our students.

When we have stopped learning about children,
we may well consider ourselves fossilized
and retire to a museum.[2]

Caroline Pratt's direct style of expression provided an instant and strong connection for me when I read her autobiography, *I Learn from Children*,[3] several years ago. What began as a satisfying read has turned into a compelling quest for more knowledge about her life and work. Unfortunately, except for the autobiography, she left little in the way of personally authored professional writings to document her career in education that spanned more than 60 years.   Even less information is available regarding her personal life. The extant information about her is contained in her own sparse writings which were more about the City and Country School she founded than they were about her. In preparing this book, I augmented the information from these personal writings with the recollections of colleagues and friends found in written accounts of their lives and personal conversations, a few scholarly documents about the work of the City and Country School, and a senior thesis and two dissertations that describe her life and work. Most of this material was published over 25 years ago. One purpose of this book is to draw this information together into a cohesive account that can enable us to better understand and relate her important contributions to education to the work we are now doing with children.

In my research, I wanted to discover how her approach to progressive education has survived, with few changes, for almost a century at the City and Country School she founded in Greenwich Village, New York. I wondered what kind of a personality enabled her to craft a philosophy and practice that has provided such a solid foundation for children's learning. I questioned how the political and social climate of the times influenced her views. And I wanted to know how her personal and professional experience was shaped by the radical thinking, activist women who were part of her professional and social circles.

These questions will be addressed in the following chapters through the reconstruction of a primarily chronological account of Caroline Pratt's life. However, a sense of place is also relevant in understanding the chronology. The moves she made to different residential locales seemed to coincide with her ideological shifts and therefore aid our understanding of her life and work. Each location provided a distinctive environment that influenced her thinking. In her hometown of Fayetteville, New York, a small traditional Victorian community, she experienced an agrarian environment where children were active participants in daily life. Schooling was not a compelling activity for her. It was something to be endured and was far less interesting than the other pursuits in which children could be engaged in and around the village.

She took her first formal pedagogical training for a career as a teacher of young children at Teachers College in New York City, beginning the year before it became affiliated with Columbia College (later Columbia University). Here she was exposed to the current thinking about teaching which was very different from what she experienced in Fayetteville. But rather than enduring what she again saw as an oppressive and impractical educational structure, she resisted it. She left the kindergartner[4] training program and switched to manual training education.[5]

She began her professional teaching in manual training in Philadelphia, Pennsylvania, at the Philadelphia Normal School for Girls. She was still not comfortable with the structured teaching methods she was imparting to future teachers. It was here, outside of her professional life, that her developing social consciousness was nurtured through contacts with a group of people whose thinking helped her to connect her new ideas about society to education.

She founded the Play School, later to become the City and Country School, after making what would become her last move to Greenwich Village in New York City. This community provided the progressive atmosphere in which she could begin her experiment in teaching children according to what she believed was a more appropriate set of methods.

Caroline's experiences in each of these places is elaborated on in the following chapters. Included in each one of the discussions of place, interpretive connections will be made to the educational (in this case, progressive) and sociocultural (in this case, feminist) contexts that shaped her thinking and her practice.

A Personal Note

Historiography, such as this biography, requires that the viewpoint of the writer be made explicit as part of the claim of validity of the written report. My viewpoint, the lens through which I understand the information available about Caroline Pratt, is colored by my experience as an educator of children, as an educator of teachers, and by my feminist view of the world. A few words of explanation are in order.

My professional background has centered primarily on the education of young children, first as a teacher, then as a teacher educator and a researcher. My training was shaped by educational applications of the qualitative research of Piaget, and later Vygotsky, and remains firmly rooted in the concept of a child-centered, active learning environment. I would have fit right in as a classroom teacher at Caroline Pratt's Play School in 1914! When I first began teaching in the late 1960s it was easier to have a child-centered classroom than it is today. The importance of play and social development, which was the focus in early childhood classrooms, was not questioned. There were many reasons for this. One was that issues of accountability were not so public then at the preschool, kindergarten, and early elementary levels. Children's development and academic progress was a matter for teachers and parents to note. Testing did not have a high-stakes value. The fact that the curriculum was less standardized and more developmentally appropriate also played a role enabling the classroom to be more child-centered. Another was that the information age had not quite exploded upon us. A consequence of these and other factors was a reorganization of curriculum, expanding "academics" into early childhood classrooms.

Working with preservice teachers and graduate students, classroom teachers who are working part time on M.Ed. degrees, we regularly discuss the need to question some of the current policies and practices in education that rob children of the opportunity to explore and experiment. The emphasis that currently permeates all levels of education places high value on standardizing the curriculum so that students will perform well on the plethora of tests that have come to measure the quality of education in our schools. Teachers must ensure that children acquire the necessary "factoids" and skills by which learning is defined and their success as educators is measured. In such an atmosphere, it is difficult to maintain a child-centered perspective. This is a great source of concern for a too-small (but growing) group of education colleagues in which I place myself.

Over the years, I have broadened my thinking about education to include an understanding of how the teaching/learning process is influenced by social and cultural contexts. This has included the idea that the social construction of teaching and learning is not a gender-neutral process, giving rise to my feminist perspective of education. I am a feminist in that I strive to deconstruct the inequity of gender relations in our culture. I see that the patriarchy in institutions of education subordinates women and creates an inequitable and, in my view, unacceptable power relationship. I am a feminist in advocating for the validity of the viewpoint and voice of women being considered on their own terms and not in comparison to that of men. This includes lived experiences and connected knowing as valid sources of knowledge. I am a feminist in that I believe that one of the strengths of the feminist movement has been to provide women the opportunity to choose the way in which they construct their lives without being bound by biological or essentialist viewpoints in their decisions. Women have the right to active agency in the shaping of their lives. These feminist viewpoints define how I write and why I write. Therefore this biography includes a feminist interpretation of the life and work of Caroline Pratt.

Two earlier biographies, both unpublished doctoral dissertations, took different views than I have taken. Maxine Hirsch, writing in 1978, used the progressive education movement as a perspective through which to view Pratt. Hirsch wrote, "it is important to describe the social and economic conditions of America prior to the turn of the century within a context of the times, and to make a number of remarks about some of the reforms that were surfacing."[6] She followed this comment with a section entitled *Progressivism and Reform* which describes these conditions and the response of social and educational reformers. She reported that the progressive movement was characterized by a tension between big business that prospered at the expense of the individual and the growing feeling of many members of the middle class of the importance of social, educational and economic reform that would benefit individuals, especially immigrants.

Patricia Carlton's dissertation is based on her interpretation of a thorough study of Pratt's ancestry. Writing in 1986, she presented a case for Pratt's ideas being influenced by the Victorian ideals to which her family subscribed. She wrote that Pratt's "family roots penetrated deep into American life and culture,"[7] beginning with her forbears who arrived in America in the first half of the seventeenth century.[8] Carlton asserted that Pratt's maternal family line was the most influential in her Victorian upbringing because of their emphasis on moral and aesthetic values.

In contrast to these two stories, I investigated possible connections to feminist organizations and individuals with whom Pratt associated when she and her lifelong partner, Helen Marot, moved to New York City. I also explored the sociopolitical context of liberalism in which Pratt and Marot were situated beginning with their friendship in Philadelphia. I don't take issue with the influence of progressivism on Pratt's educational practice; however, I do question the strength of the connection that is often made between Pratt and Dewey. That, however, is a topic I will deal with in more detail later in Chapter Six, "Enacting a Radical Philosophy." I do take issue with Carlton's Victorian interpretation and will present evidence in Chapter Two, "Growing up in Fayetteville," from her own writing that indicates that very early on Pratt behaved differently than typical Victorian women in Fayetteville.

These accounts of Pratt's life were written before the inclusion of an author's personal lens became common practice in preparing historiographic biographical writing. Not knowing the perspectives of Hirsch and Carlton, it is really impossible to comment definitively on the validity of the interpretations these writers made. In contrast, I am writing with the experience of qualitative historiography and feminist research practice behind me that requires the presentation of my biases. Therefore if the reader accepts my perspectives/biases, my story about Caroline Pratt may have somewhat more credibility. When viewed through a feminist lens of interpretation, I believe Pratt's contributions to educational thought have more power than when only a progressive or Victorian interpretation is used. The feminist lens adds a missing dimension that influenced a number of progressive women educators at the turn of the twentieth century. Nevertheless, it is ultimately up to the reader to judge the value of using a feminist analysis. It is important to make sure that the researcher's bias is clear, up front, so that the reader can decide for herself or himself whether or not the account is credible.

Significance of the Book

I became "acquainted" with Caroline Pratt through her writings more than ten years ago. I made a strong connection with her thinking about teaching young children when I read her autobiography as part of my quest to understand the historical underpinnings of early childhood education. As I have journeyed through her writings and the writings of others about her and the school she founded, I have come to know and respect this complex woman who lived and worked in a time of dramatic social and educational change. She had an unwavering commitment to learning about how children should be educated and for providing the best possible environment to meet children's individual purposes. She did not allow her vision to be constrained by the traditional social and educational practices of the early twentieth century. She gathered a circle of strong women (and some men) into her personal and professional circles who supported her ideals. Her life can be a model for all education professionals, not only those who work with young children.

Pratt is part of an education legacy that reminds us that we have choices in our practice. There are methods that have been demonstrated as being effective in the past that we can look to for guidance, inspiration, and validation. Robert Levin declares that the historical record provides data about tried but neglected approaches to resolve important educational dilemmas facing us today and about track records of many elements of today's restructuring programs.[9] Relating this idea specifically to Pratt, Barbara Beatty writes, "Caroline Pratt's and Harriet Johnson's experiments in preschool education in Greenwich Village before World War I provided enormous quantities of information about educational environments for young children. Their extensive observations of children's play, particularly with blocks and the learning materials they developed, became the basis of modern nursery school curricula that focuses on free expression and creativity."[10]

An early childhood researcher, Blythe Hinitz, talks about the value of historical writing to bring the history of education, childhood education, and child development closer to our lives.[11] Such action could counter the ahistorical nature of the profession of education. Admittedly, the push for accountability plays a part in the forward focus of educators who constantly seek the newest methods and materials, the latest thinking about teaching and learning to use with their students. Many feel forced into a "what can I do on Monday morning?" mindset which results in superficial evaluation of methods and materials and omits consideration of their origins or "track records." But part of the definition of a profession is that it has a history. If the history of education, including curriculum and pedagogical development, was highlighted more in the training of teachers, the frantic and frustrating pendulum swings of educational practice might be somewhat tempered by the knowledge of previous experience.

Finally, this telling of Caroline Pratt's story extends the idea of documenting the contributions of women leaders called for by Susan Semel and Alan Sadovnik in order that "their names [will] be more than historical footnotes or asides in the history of progressive education."[12] And as Kathleen Weiler so elegantly states about feminist writing, it provides witness to women teachers' valuable and unrecognized work.[13] The story retrieves and celebrates our female heritage and "creates...a tradition that can sustain women personally."[14] For me that statement can include sustaining like-minded men as well. Men who support feminist ideals or declare themselves to be feminist are linked to this tradition. Because the boundaries between the personal and professional identities of educators are often blurred, I also connect Weiler's statement to sustaining oneself professionally.

I want to recognize at the outset of this book that some readers of Caroline Pratt's life story may argue that making a distinction between her as a feminist practitioner or a progressive practitioner is unnecessary. After all, both feminist and progressive practices can easily be considered examples of good educational practice. But that argument is irrelevant in this context. The importance of using a feminist lens to understand Caroline Pratt lies in the argument that without women's history and a feminist consciousness, the achievements of women in public and professional life can easily be erased. Unless women's part in the development of progressive education is recorded, that influence will be lost to our understanding. While men such as Colonel Francis Parker, John Dewey, and William Heard Kilpatrick are well established as the primary exponents of the progressive movement in education, the work of Caroline Pratt and similar female educators also has a place in the progressive education record.[15] Margaret Naumberg, Marietta Johnson, and Elsie Ripley Clapp are examples of the women who founded schools based on progressive principles and in the process refined and expanded current educational thinking. Their work provides important examples of experientially grounded practices of progressive education. Finally, using a gendered lens to understand Pratt's life and work recognizes and makes explicit the role of the sociocultural context of gender in constructing human knowledge. A variety of women activists and men and women artists who had creative approaches to their lives and work were part of the social and professional milieu that shaped the educator Pratt became. This book then, will include exploration of the connections between Caroline Pratt and both progressive education and early twentieth century feminism in order to add depth to our understanding of her as a person and of her important work in education.

The Progressive Context

The progressive context of Caroline Pratt's life and work encompasses both the Progressive Movement in the United States and related changes in educational thought and practices which were collected under the umbrella of progressive education. American Progressivism includes the period between about 1890 and the beginning of World War II. Progressive Education was a force in the American educational system beginning at the turn of the twentieth century through about 1955, and there still remain adherents to its ideals.

Progressive Movement. This was the name given to the remarkable metamorphosis of a young agricultural United States into a maturing industrial nation.[16] While the Progressive Movement was never unitary in concept or practice, there were some common elements contributing to the upheaval in society during this metamorphosis that contemporary writers describe.[17] They include the rapid increase in urbanization, as a result of the decline in agrarian society and the rise of industrialization; and the dramatic increase in immigration to the United States. Other elements were a general reaction to the moral oppression of Puritan restraint[18] as well as to "aesthetic superficiality"[19] associated with the Victorian period.

While the effects of the Progressive Movement were apparent in many aspects of American society, they were particularly evident in cities where the contrasts of wealth and poverty were clearly seen. These effects have been described as both positive and negative. The main "curse of industrialization" was seen as a change in the structure of the American family and in the fabric of communities resulting in a lack of connection and an increase of social alienation. This change was at the root of many of the social ills that were described as being in need of amelioration. Further, newly arrived workers were outside the mainstream of American life because of their different customs and language, a situation that also contributed to a lack of connection within communities.

Despite these troubling social conditions, or maybe because of them, a characteristic of Progressivism was a newfound social consciousness, spurred on by the settlement house movement recently brought to the United States from England. The plight of the poor and of immigrants was not seen as their inevitable lot, and therefore social programs based on education were instituted by settlement houses to address the particular needs of the people they served. Sweatshop working environments for women and children, slum living conditions, and corruption in politics were examples of the focus of reform-minded citizens, settlement workers, and journalists.

The social consciousness of the period spawned a feeling of optimism toward change through individual effort. Individuals could make a difference through their participation in democracy. Boyd Bode refers to this phenomenon as the rise of the common man to participation in what had previously been a social and cultural heritage from which he was excluded. People, rather than faceless institutions, could remake the world.[20]

However, after the flush of public spirit that accompanied the end of World War I, exhaustion and frustration surfaced. According to some historians, this was the result of people realizing that all their work and sacrifice for the ideals the country had fought for were not being realized. A different kind of progressivism developed that "asked somewhat less of social reform and more of the conditions that would make for originality in the expression of individuals."[21] Many progressives believed that individuals who were able to develop their creative potential in environments such as the progressive schools afforded, were necessary for the development of a democratic society.

The arts were also looked to as an avenue toward overcoming the bleakness and spiritual aridity of the industrial revolution. This aspect of Progressivism was less focused on social reform than progressive thought had been at the turn of the century. Rather, the emphasis of this kind of progressivism was on conditions that would foster individual expression.[22]

Progressive Education. There has always been a deep-seated belief in the United States in the power of education to improve the lot of individuals and as a consequence improve the larger society. So it is not surprising that education was seen as a primary means of addressing many of the goals of Progressivism. Specifically, education in the first two decades of the twentieth century became a tool of social reform in such areas as education of immigrants, improving American culture, emphasizing individual development, realizing the social purpose of life,[23] promoting suffrage for women, and advocating for the rights of children.

But schools, in their turn-of-the-century state, were not up to such a task. They were housed in crumbling buildings, full of overcrowded classrooms and outdated teaching materials. Many reformers saw education, delivered in its traditional passive, regurgitative way, as counterproductive to the urgent need for social change. The traditional pedagogy with its reliance on drill and memorization of disconnected information was stultifying. The "sit-still methods" in "screwed down desks"[24] would no longer meet the needs of the new pedagogy. Indeed, a number of progressive schools were founded, including Caroline Pratt's Play School, in direct response to the dissatisfaction with these educational conditions. This dissatisfaction was expressed not only by educators who founded the schools, but also by many parents who were instrumental in establishing schools with alternative practices.[25]

In describing examples of progressive schools in *Schools of Tomorrow*[26] John Dewey and his daughter, Evelyn Dewey, hearken back to the work of Rousseau, Pestalozzi, and Froebel to trace the antecedents of the so-called new education. Each innovator saw childhood as a distinct period of life, one which the child had a right to enjoy without imposition of adult-based pedagogy. Education was seen as a process of development of the mind and the body. Each man had a different emphasis (Rousseau: the importance of the child's interaction with the natural environment; Pestalozzi: the value of children's social interactions; Froebel: the role of the intellectual and metaphysical systems in the developmental process) but all respected the child's ability to be a participant in the development process.

So from the beginning, it is clear that Progressive Education, while sharing a number of commonalities, was no more unitary in its ideals than those of the Progressive Movement. They were pluralistic and sometimes even seemed contradictory. For example, Bode, reflecting on 20 years of progressive education in *Progressive Education at the Crossroads*, pointed out that schools emphasize freedom while attaching importance to guidance and direction of the child. The individual is central, yet the competitive character of society is criticized, which would indicate a rejection of the philosophy of individualism. Learning by doing is championed, yet physical activity tapers off in classrooms for older children. Progressive educators both reject and employ defined or structured curriculum models. Higher education is denigrated as the "citadel of its enemy," yet the chief business of many schools is preparing its students to enter these citadels.[27]

Within these contradictions, however, classrooms/schools that were considered progressive possessed some common characteristics. These common characteristics included the following practices:

- Curricula were child-centered based in the child's purpose for activity.
- The teacher was seen as a creator of learning environments and a guide in the learning process.
- A sense of community was important to develop within classrooms, and within a school.
- The process of learning was emphasized through exploration and experimentation more than the products of learning.

- A variety of arts for both creative imagination and self-expression were emphasized.
- Innovative subjects, including manual training, domestic science, and nature study, were a part of the curriculum (or activities if the term "curriculum" was considered too restrictive).

Caroline Pratt's description of the Play School's program was in accord with these common characteristics, "The attempt in the Play School has been to place the children in an environment through which by experiment with that environment they may become self-educated."[28] Later, she elaborated on this basic idea in a symposium published in *The New Republic* in 1930:

The new types of curriculum, as shown in what are termed, "progressive" schools, have in common more and more opportunities for experiencing inquiring, experimenting, and less stress on subject matter and memorizing. More attention is given to the processes of learning and study of growth habits by teachers and less to teaching and the development of teaching methods. Experimenting means experimentation *by* children and not experimentation *with* children. In fact, the zeal for teaching is giving place to the effort to provide an environment in which children can gradually take over their own learning processes.[29]

Another way in which Caroline Pratt's school was consistent with then current thinking about progressive education was in its emphasis on the creative arts. In New York City, Greenwich Village was the center of expressionism that was flourishing in the bohemian and intellectual enclaves of the U.S. major cities. Creative artists in all fields were attracted to this neighborhood and were delighted to send their children to a school that emphasized the kind of individual expression that they were trying to accomplish with their own art. They were willing to take a chance on Pratt's unconventional methods which undoubtedly strengthened her position on the place of creative arts in her curriculum. She wrote that:

the essence of good teaching is to see the child not as an artisan, following a blueprint against which his actions or behavior can be checked, but as a creative artist thinking though his problems. He starts out with an idea, to be sure, but it is an idea which he needs to clarify through his method of dealing with it...such a method is a method of thinking.[30]

The issue of curriculum was a major one that occupied both exponents and critics of progressive education. How could a school based on the interests of the students have a curriculum that consisted of traditional school subjects?

J.L. Meriam struggled with this issue in his small progressive school at the University of Missouri. After some years of experimentation, "a four-fold organization of curriculum activities and materials was developed: observation, play, stories, and handwork."[31] Accordingly, the school day was divided into four 90-minute periods. This flexible arrangement contrasted with the rigid 10- to 30-minute periods of instruction found in traditional schools. Caroline Pratt's organization of curriculum, discussed in more detail in Chapter Seven, included similar broad activity-based areas: play activities, practical activities, skills or techniques, and enrichment of experiences (later known as organization of information).

Another feature of progressive curriculum was the idea of projects which integrated traditional "school subjects" (reading, math, social studies, science, and the arts) around "wholehearted purposeful activity proceeding in a social environment."[32] William H. Kilpatrick is best known for popularizing the idea which was adapted in a variety of ways in progressive schools. At the City and Country School, the project approach took the form of the jobs curriculum for the older elementary students. (See Chapter Seven.)

Lawrence Cremin, in his analysis of progressive education, termed Pratt's application of expressionism the "pedagogical version of the expressionist credo."[33] His writing, and that of other leading documenters of Progressive Education, have firmly established Caroline Pratt's place in the forefront of the private school progressive movement.[34] Her school can be described as one that "best reflects the tenets of the progressive ideal."[35]

The Feminist Context

As the twentieth century began, noticeable shifts in women's place in society became a great concern for many males in a variety of professional areas. Some women resented the restraints that the Victorian ideal of woman had placed upon them, and they took it upon themselves to become educated, eschew marriage and family, and seek professional work in territories that men had dominated. These actions were contrary to deeply rooted views in our culture of the differences between the sexes and the intellectual inferiority of women. "Scientific" information as well as injunctions based on "common knowledge" and "the testimony of literature" was used by "experts" to support views that maintained the superiority of men.[36]

The physical inferiority of women was also touted by "experts." For example, Carroll Smith-Rosenberg reports that nineteenth-century male physicians considered the uniquely female aspects of woman's physiology (menstruation, pregnancy, childbirth, lactation, menopause) were central to all of a woman's physical and social experiences. Women were seen as fragile creatures dominated by their reproductive processes. To thwart the requirements of the reproductive organs was to court disease, insanity, and death.[37]

In addition to the above "knowledge" about women, another ploy developed to keep them from getting into the wrong path and destroying America's social fabric. This was to channel the education women sought into the areas of homemaking and nurturing, to prepare them for the situations to which they were most naturally suited. It was believed that rigorous work and study could endanger the health of women and jeopardize their child-producing abilities. "Women's body and soul are made for maternity...even if she does not realize it, her whole nature demands first of all children to love."[38] This approach to education, it was felt, would stem the tide of declining birthrate, rising divorce rate, the increasing number of women in the labor force, and those seeking higher education. Such was the atmosphere into which Feminism, then a new word recently imported from Europe, was introduced. It is important to note, however, that women's issues had been debated for years before in terms of the right to vote and own property.

As is the case today, Feminism (early uses of the word were capitalized) at the turn of the twentieth century lacked unified, widely held, mutually shared understandings. But according to one women's historian, Nancy Cott, women's efforts in the 1910s and 1920s both "laid the groundwork and exposed the fault lines of modern feminism."[39] She asserted that ideas about identity and group consciousness that characterized early Feminism as well as the paradoxes which came to define modern feminism are still evident. These paradoxes include an emphasis on sexual equality that includes sexual difference, a move to women's individual freedoms achieved through mobilization of sexual solidarity, and gender consciousness while calling for the elimination of prescribed gender roles. "What characterized the feminism of the 1910s was its very multifaceted constitution, the fact that several strands were all loudly voiced and mutually recognized as part of the same phenomenon of female avant-garde self-assertion."[40] The strands in this multifaceted conception were women's claim for full citizenship, equal wages for equal work, psychic freedom and spiritual autonomy, sexual liberation and the independence of wives.

Another interpreter of feminism, Beatrice Forbes-Robertson Hale, writing in 1914, emphasized the ideas of choice for women, the potential power of women's united voice speaking for social change, and the recognition that women's heretofore unrecognized talents were needed to advance society.[41] Obviously none of these ideas were new, but it was the combination, named as Feminism, and containing an open-endedness and acceptance of internal contradictions around which its adherents congregated.

A significant influence on Feminism in New York was the Heterodoxy Club[42] that met in Greenwich Village between 1912 and 1940. It was an organization of women who consciously regarded themselves as pioneers in forming a "new" feminist theory and practice. Their focus was not primarily on the issues of suffrage that related to the legal and political emancipation of women, but dealt instead with ideas about sex-solidarity, sexual emancipation, and a search for female role models and for a female based system of values and ethics.[43] The personal and private dimensions of liberation were paramount. Speaking to a public forum in 1914, author and suffrage leader Rose Emmet Young articulated the personal dimension that virtually all of the club members valued: "To me, feminism means that woman wants to develop her own womanhood. It means that she wants to push on to the finest, fullest, freest expression of herself. She wants to be an individual....The freeing of the individuality of woman does not mean original sin, it means the finding of her own soul."[44] It was clear that personal choice and self-determination were hallmarks of the Heterodites' thinking.

In a series of well-turned phrases, playwright (and husband of Heterodoxy member Fola LaFollette) George Middleton described his sense of Feminism as "a spiritual attitude. It means trouble; trouble means agitation, agitation means movement; movement means life, life means adjustment and readjustment—so does feminism."[45] This description captures the openness and energy of Feminism, a feeling of moving forward in one's life. It also hints at the challenge that society will have in accommodating feminist thinking.

Caroline Pratt was not a member of the Heterodoxy Club, but several of her friends and professional colleagues were active participants in the organization. Fola LaFollette was associated with the City and Country School between 1926 and 1930. She taught French and English, as well as being in charge of the school library. Elisabeth Irwin, the founder of another Greenwich Village progressive school, the Little Red Schoolhouse, and her partner Katharine Anthony, were both Heterodoxy members. Ida Rauh, a sculptor, actress and founder of the Provincetown Players, who had a reputation as a social agitator, was a friend and onetime neighbor in Greenwich Village. Anne Herendeen, a writer and editor, was also a friend. Although Caroline Pratt's philosophy and practice was not intentionally feminist, the influence of relationships with these women and with her lifelong companion, Helen Marot, a leader in labor organization and investigation, cannot be discounted. These women were clearly enacting as well as advocating for the advancement of the new feminism of the twentieth century. Finally, because she chose to live in Greenwich Village when she moved to New York, I am assuming that Pratt was open to the liberal thinking that she found within her neighborhood.

As connections to feminism are made throughout the book, it is important to point out that these connections are to early twentieth-century Feminism, as described by authors such as Nancy Cott, Beatrice Forbes-Robertson Hale, Kate Wittenstein and Judith Schwarz. Although similarities in feminist theory and practice are evident across the years, I have carefully tried to avoid applying modern feminist concepts in my interpretation of the life of Caroline Pratt and the women with whom she associated.

Notes

1. ILFC, 70.
2. ILFC, 68.
3. Harper & Row, 1970, originally published in hardcover by Simon & Schuster in 1948. All citations are taken from the 1970 edition of *I Learn from Children*.

4. This term was used at the time to identify kindergarten teachers. Nowadays it refers to a student in kindergarten.

5. ILFC, 11.

6. Hirsch, "Caroline Pratt and the City and Country School: 1914-1945," 2.

7. Carlton, "Caroline Pratt: A Biography," 18.

8. Ibid., footnote, 27.

9. Levin, "The Debate over Schooling."

10. Beatty, *Preschool Education in America*, 42.

11. Lascarides and Hinitz, *History of Early Childhood Education*.

12. Sadovnik and Semel, *Founding Mothers and Others*, 259.

13. Weiler, "Reflections on Writing a History of Women Teachers."

14. Asher, DeSalvo, and Ruddick, *Between Women*, xxiii.

15. This record is being advanced by recent publications such as Sadovnik and Semel's edited volume, *Founding Mothers and Others*, and Stack's biography, *Elsie Ripley Clapp (1879-1965)*.

16. Cremin, Shannon, and Townsend, *History of Teachers College Columbia University*, 5.

17. More exhaustive accounts of the Progressive Movement and its effect on education can be found in Cremin, *The Transformation of the School: Progressivism in American Education 1876-1957*, and Beck, "Progressive Education and American Progressivism: Caroline Pratt."

18. Beck, "Progressive Education and American Progressivism."

19. Ibid., 130.

20. Bode, *Progressive Education at the Crossroads*.

21. Beck, "Progressive Education and American Progressivism," 130.

22. Ibid.

23. Bode, *Progressive Education at the Crossroads*, 10.

24. ILFC, 1, 167.

25. See Marcus, "The Founding of American Private Progressive Schools 1912-1921," for an analysis of the reasons for the founding of nine progressive schools, including the Play School.

26. Dewey and Dewey, *Schools of Tomorrow*.

27. Bode, *Progressive Education at the Crossroads*, 10.

28. CP and L. Deming, Experimental Schools, Bulletin #3, 23.

29. CP, "Two Basic Principles of Education," 172.

30. CP, *Before Books*.

31. Rugg and Schumacher, *The Child-centered School*, 41. Meriam's school was also described in Dewey and Dewey, *Schools of Tomorrow*.

32. William H. Kilpatrick. "The Project Method," *Teachers College Record* XIX, quoted in Cremin, *The Transformation of the School*, 217.

33. Cremin, *The Transformation of the School*, 206.

34. See Robert Beck, "American Progressive Education 1875-1930," and "Progressive Education and American Progressivism: Caroline Pratt. Teachers College Record; Lawrence Cremin, *The Transformation of the School: Progressivism in American Education 1876-1957*; Patricia A. Graham, *From Arcady to Academe*; and John and Evelyn Dewey, *Schools of Tomorrow*, for their analyses of Caroline Pratt's progressive school practice.

35. Dewey and Dewey, *Schools of Tomorrow*.

36. Seller, "G. Stanley Hall and Edward Thorndike on the Education of Women," 370.
37. Smith-Rosenberg, *Disorderly Conduct*, 23.
38. Ibid., footnote 6, 374.
39. Cott, *The Grounding of Modern Feminism*, 4.
40. Ibid., 49.
41. Hale, *What Women Want*.
42. Wittenstein, "The Heterodoxy Club and American Feminism, 1912-1930."
43. Ibid.
44. Schwarz, *The Radical Feminists of Heterodoxy*, 25.
45. Wittenstein, "The Heterodoxy Club," 50. As the husband of Heterodoxy member Fola La Follette, George Middleton's knowledge of feminism was more than academic.

PHOTOS. BY SMITH, FAYETTEVILLE.

SEYMOUR PRATT.

NANCY PRATT.

Figure 2. Caroline Pratt's paternal grandparents.
Figure 3. Lizzie Pratt, Caroline's older sister.
Figure 4. Caroline Pratt's childhood home, Fayetteville, NY.

CHAPTER TWO

Growing up in Fayetteville

I began the adventure innocently enough when at sixteen
I became the teacher of a one-room school not far from Fayetteville[1]

WITH THIS SIMPLE AND DIRECT STATEMENT, Caroline Pratt introduced her autobiography, *I Learn from Children*. However, the simplicity of the written statement masks the breadth and depth of her experience as a progressive educator and a radical social thinker, the experience that this book is designed to chronicle.

The one-room district school in Pratt's Falls in the town of Pompey, 15 miles from Fayetteville, was where her teaching "adventure" began. (Coincidently, the school was near where her great-great-grandfather Manoah Pratt had established one of the first mills in Onondaga County.) She took on this summer term teaching job at the suggestion of her relative, Homer Pratt. She recalled, "It was my great-uncle Homer's idea, possibly born of the neighbors' endorsement, 'Carrie was always good with children'."[2] It was the summer of 1884, the summer after her seventeenth birthday. There is no documentation of what or how she taught that summer school, but since she had no formal knowledge of teaching practice, it is safe to assume that she taught as she had been taught. We can only speculate about how the independent nature she possessed might have shaped this first teaching experience. Based on her later recollections of how she felt she learned best, she may well have included some active, out-of-the-classroom experiences for her students along with the disciplined drill and memorization exercises she probably felt compelled to conduct.

Family

Caroline,[3] called Carrie in her childhood and youth, was born on May 13, 1867, the third of four children of Henry and Lydia (Rowley) Pratt. Her sister Elizabeth Sophia was born December 21, 1859, and her brother John Davis on December 23, 1861. The last sibling, her younger brother, Henry Rowley, was born on October 30, 1871.

Her birthplace of Fayetteville, a few miles east of Syracuse, was a town of about 1,500 inhabitants. First known as The Corners, it was founded in 1791. Later it became Manlius Four Corners and in 1818 was changed by the U.S. Post Office to Fayetteville in honor of the Marquis de Lafayette, the French Revolutionary War hero. Lafayette was to visit the area in 1825 to mark the opening of the Erie Canal.[4] The canal ran just a mile from Fayetteville and was an important stimulant to its early economic development. The village of Fayetteville was incorporated in 1844.

Carrie's forbears, from both her mother's and father's families, were among the first European-American homesteaders in Onondaga County. They engaged over various generations in farming, lumbering, milling, and later building contracting, acquiring financial success and attaining solid middle class status. Both her grandfather and father assumed civic responsibilities including holding public office in the community.[5]

Carlton's descriptions of Carrie's parents, Henry and Lydia Pratt, fit the conventional roles of the Victorian family.[6] By the time of Carrie's birth, her family had attained a good social reputation partly because both her parents' families had such long standing in the area. In particular, Carrie's paternal grandfather Seymour was seen as a pillar of the community. He had large landholdings and ran a number of successful businesses. Henry Pratt, a Civil War veteran, was also a businessman, and was respected for his personal charm and wit. He enjoyed good times that included hunting and fishing excursions. He often organized and participated in civic parades. An active supporter of the Democratic Party, his politics were in opposition of those of his Republican brothers. The fact that Henry was not a churchgoer did not seem to diminish his status in the community.

Lydia Pratt's demeanor was typical of Victorian womanhood. Described as possessing a sweet and gentle character, "kindly cheer," and aesthetic sensibilities, she was known as a charming and genteel woman. As expected, her sphere of influence was primarily family, church, and charity.[7] She was active in social and self-improvement clubs that were popular during the end of the nineteenth century and entertained graciously, according to the local Fayetteville newspaper, *The Weekly Recorder*. It was undoubtedly she who arranged for the baptism of Carrie and her older brother and sister in the Trinity Episcopal Church on March 12, 1868.

Despite the conventional Victorian nature of Carrie's family, there is no evidence that they discouraged her from her development as an active, self-confident youngster. She was raised in a house on Elm Street, close to the place where her grandfather had put down family roots.[8] She grew up as an independent, capable individual. There is ample indication that she valued those qualities in herself and that others saw them in her as well. She related that, "at ten, my great aunt used to say that I could turn a team of horses and a wagon in less space than a grown man needed to do it."[9]

Schooling

The rural environment of Fayetteville lent itself to children participating in the daily activities necessary to the functioning of the community. However, that expected participation was not always valued by the children. Many years after leaving Fayetteville, Caroline recalled in her autobiography the important influence of these activities on her philosophy of teaching and learning.

> Again and again in my life of learning from children I have remembered my own childhood, and that eager desire to help grown-ups in grown-up work only to be given the lowliest and least interesting chores to do. How happily I would have washed the pots and pans if I had a hand in the cooking that was done in them.[10]

Caroline had fonder memories of active, independent play which she shared with her friends:

> The things that I remember as a child are the long rovings in the woods on Saturdays, the farm where I spent a brief period every summer, the village 'baby hole' where the boys learned to swim and which I was allowed to visit properly guarded when it wasn't in use...the dramatic play we carried on in the 'back yard.' These were the times I lived during my childhood.[11]

These growing up experiences mirror the ideas of interpreters of progressive educational practice who characterize it as an attempt to capture in urban areas these qualities of the teaching/learning process that are found in small rural agriculturally based communities.[12] Not coincidentally, John Dewey's progressive philosophy was influenced by his rural upbringing in Vermont. He wrote that "we cannot overlook the importance for educational purposes of the close and intimate acquaintance got with nature at first hand, with real things and materials, with the actual processes of their manipulation, and the knowledge of their social necessities and uses."[13]

In sharp contrast, schooling was seemingly a somewhat dreaded necessary evil and "consisted of the mechanics of the three Rs and a bit of information about far away and long ago."[14] With Caroline's characteristic directness, she described her learnings as "unwanted, unrelated, and delivered in an indigestible format."[15] "We learned to sit still and to dispose of what was handed out to us in our own individual way" while waiting for the recess period, then the "noon release" and the final closing of school.[16] In another recollection she reported, "Just as it has always been, the children begin to live when they make their escape from school."[17] Her use of "release" and "escape" in her writing effectively conveys the constraint she remembered feeling as a youngster in school. Although one's memories contain both recollections and reconstructions of past events, these memories of Caroline's dramatically foreshadow the kind of thinking that shaped her educational philosophy.

She and her classmates managed to survive the oppressive system of schooling of her day, and *The Weekly Recorder* of June 24, 1886, noted the graduation of Carrie's high school class. She had passed the Regents Advanced Examination in algebra, physics, geometry, and political economy. Part of her survival may be credited to the fact that she enjoyed reading (mostly outside of school, however).

Her early active, practical learning experiences in Fayetteville left a lasting impression and undoubtedly have contributed to her later ideas about progressive education. The kinds of experiences in which Caroline and her friends could be out and about, learning on their own, rather than in a classroom with its sometimes stultifying structure, were the ones that she believed provided the best opportunities to learn.

Young Adulthood

The next year found her at home following the conventional practice for young unmarried women. She undoubtedly helped her mother with her father's care. Since 1884, an illness that had overtaken him had become more severe and he became increasingly unable to care for himself.

However, in the fall of 1887 Caroline was asked to accept a position teaching first grade in the village school. The school population had burgeoned and the school board decided to hire another teacher to cover the increase in enrollment. While there is no direct record of Caroline's thinking process, it is probable that one reason for her taking a job was to supplement the family income necessitated by her father's declining health and inability to work. It may have been that she was pressed into service as a teacher, rather than making a conscious decision to do so. She didn't write about having a career until after about three years of teaching. It wasn't until 1891, she recalled, that she gave some focused thought to the idea of what kind of a career she might consider for herself. For a young woman to consciously choose a profession was very un-Victorian behavior.

Historical records of Fayetteville place a lot of emphasis on the intellectual and social clubs that flourished in the late 1880s. Records of those club activities were reported exhaustively in the newspaper, *The Weekly Recorder*. Since Caroline didn't belong to these clubs, she didn't make the papers. She didn't follow the traditional path of young women socializing even though both her mother and sister were active members in a variety of organizations. Instead, as Carlton pointed out, Caroline was active in a club for lawn tennis and she attended the Chautauqua Literary and Scientific Circle, which held meetings with readings and discussions in the subjects of history and government.[18]

A record of her sister Lizzie (Elizabeth) being able to play the piano and do fancy needlework exists,[19] but it seems that Caroline didn't engage in such pursuits typical of young Victorian women. In describing Caroline as a young woman of 20, Carlton reported that Caroline didn't dress the same way as her peers. She did not wear the decorative rosette and ribbon or dainty lace cuffs some women wore to add a touch of femininity to their silk dresses.[20] The contemporary

Victorian behavior and styles seemed not to influence her. One might theorize that the roots of her (unnamed) feminism began to develop in her rejection of some of the Victorian behaviors to which she was exposed.

Fayetteville resident Matilda Joslyn Gage's influence on Carrie's thinking is also open to speculation. The Gage family lived in Fayetteville from 1854 until Mrs. Gage's death in 1898. Since her youngest daughter was six years older than Caroline and married in 1882, four years before Carrie graduated from high school, it is unlikely that the girls had direct contact, even though the families lived nearby one another. Mrs. Gage was described as an ardent feminist, but in retrospect, was more accurately a leader in the woman movement, a precursor to what was labeled Feminism in the early part of the twentieth century. The woman movement denotes the many ways women moved out of the home to initiate charity work, temperance, social welfare, civic rights, social freedoms, higher education, remunerative occupations, and the ballot. The label of woman movement implied a singular thinking, that all women have one cause. Mrs. Gage was closely associated with Susan B. Anthony and Elizabeth Cady Stanton and their campaigns for women's suffrage, and was a frequent contributor to the Fayetteville weekly newspaper, writing about women's issues. It may be more likely that any influence from this important feminist came to Carrie through reading about Mrs. Gage's activities in the newspaper as well as reading articles she contributed.

A tragedy befell the Pratt family in May 1889, less than a week before Caroline turned 22. Her father took his own life. His deteriorating health began to manifest itself in mental depression. The mental decline was partially the result of the pain he suffered and partially from the strong medication he took to relieve the pain. The disease, known today as locomotor ataxia, was then called creeping paralysis or *tabes dorsalis*. It involves progressive degeneration of the nerve fibers of the spinal cord that causes intense shooting pains and progressive paralysis. The disease may not develop for 10 to 20 years after the initial infection that can be caused by a spinal cord injury or infection (e.g., syphilis).[21]

Under the influence of depression and pain, Henry Pratt threatened to take his life, so his wife's Uncle Homer came to watch over Pratt to prevent him from doing so. The two newspapers that reported the tragedy gave conflicting accounts of Pratt's final hour the evening of May 7. While *The Syracuse Journal*, May 8, 1889, reported that Homer Pratt was attending his nephew, *The* (Fayetteville) *Weekly Recorder*, May 9, 1889, reported that Mrs. Pratt was with her husband. Both newspapers indicated that Pratt had been left alone for a few minutes during which time he cut his throat and fell to the floor. Hearing a noise, Mrs. Pratt (or Homer Pratt, depending on which newspaper you read) hurried back to find Pratt on the floor in a pool of blood. He had taken his life by making three razor cuts in his throat.

Henry Pratt's funeral was private, with only family, intimate friends, and army comrades invited. However, the large representation of citizens who gathered, according to the May 16, 1889, issue of *The Weekly Recorder*, attested to the respect for Henry Pratt's memory and the sympathy friends and neighbors felt for the bereaved family. A group of fellow Civil War officers from Pratt's military unit, the 10th New York Cavalry, served as pallbearers.

Both Caroline and her mother took extended trips after Henry Pratt's death. Caroline went to visit relatives in Philadelphia and Lydia Pratt went on a vacation with close friends. Both trips probably provided needed respite after the intensive care Henry Pratt required during the final period of his illness.

Caroline continued to teach in Fayetteville for the next three years. Newspaper records of school events included mention of Caroline's class. Two records seemed to foreshadow Caroline's later teaching practices of actively engaging her students and connecting the curriculum to their experiences. The first was her use of small colored cubes to work with numbers in order to fix the association between symbol and reality in a child's mind.[22] The second was a play presented at the school's Anniversary Exercises program. It was called "The Children's Strike" and was presented at a time of nation-wide strikes.[23] At an Arbor Day program in June 1892, her class rendered a song, "Marching for Arbor." "The intricate marching...all and each were performed without a break or halt either in step or in singing."[24] This was to be her last year of teaching in Fayetteville because she was accepted at Teachers College in New York for the start of the fall term in 1892. Except for a brief period in the summer of 1894 between graduating from Teachers College and beginning her job in Philadelphia, it was her last year of residence in the family home. There is no record of her returning to Fayetteville, even for a visit.

Notes

1. LFC, xvi.
2. ILFC, xvi. The Manlius town historian, Ms. Barbara Rivette, suggested to me (personal correspondence, March 17, 2003) that in Carrie's day the summer term was usually attended by girls and younger children because boys were working on the farms. School trustees usually tried to get a male teacher for the winter term that the "bigger" boys attended when farm work was less demanding.
3. In contrast to most biographical accounts in which the subject is referred to using last name only, I have chosen to use a feminist form in which the subject's first name is the primary referent in sections documenting the early years of her life and in discussing her personal life. I have used Miss Pratt in writing about her professional life in New York. There are precedents for the use of the first name in other biographical writing of feminist authors, such as *Lucy Sprague Mitchell: The Making of a Modern Woman* (Antler, 1987), *Harriet Stanton Blatch and the Winning of Woman Suffrage* (Ellen Carol Dubois, 1997) and *To Herland and Beyond: The Life and Work of Charlotte Perkins Gilman* (Ann J. Lane, 1990).
4. There is an often repeated but unverifiable incident associated with Lafayette's visit. As the story goes, a royal demonstration to welcome Lafayette was held as the boats made their way up the canal. During the celebration activities, a young boy was accidentally wounded by a cannon ball, and he later died. Upon hearing of the tragic event, Lafayette sent a sum of gold to the bereaved, widowed mother. Initially, the town honored Lafayette by dedicating the post office to his memory. [Journal by Miriam Collins, 1896-1900, FFL, quoted in Hirsch, pp. 18, 19]
5. See Carlton, "Caroline Pratt: A Biography," for extensive information regarding Pratt's family genealogy and activity in Fayetteville and the surrounding communities.
6. Ibid., 55.
7. "Most 18th and 19th century women lived within a world bounded by home, church and the institution of visiting—that endless trooping of women to one another's homes for social purposes." Smith-Rosenberg, *Disorderly Conduct: Visions of Gender in Victorian America*, 61.
8. Carlton, "Caroline Pratt: A Biography," 57.
9. ILFC, xv.
10. Ibid., 8.
11. Pratt and Stanton, *Before Books*, 13.
12. Cremin, *The Transformation of the School*.
13. Dewey, *The School and Society*, 23-4.
14. ILFC, xvi.

15. Ibid., 6.
16. Pratt and Stanton, *Before Books*, 12.
17. Ibid., 13.
18. Carlton, "Caroline Pratt: A Biography," 125.
19. Ibid.
20. Ibid., 118.
21. *Encyclopedia Britannica* online, 2006.
22. ILFC, 52.
23. Carlton, "Caroline Pratt: A Biography," 128.
24. *Weekly Recorder*, quoted in Carlton, "Caroline Pratt: A Biography," 138.

CHAPTER THREE

Teachers College, New York: Formal Education Training

*To study at Teachers College
was considered quite an advanced thing to do,
in the year 1892...*[1]

CAROLINE PRATT APPARENTLY INQUIRED into attending Teachers College a year before the year of her enrollment, because the letter below asked whether acting-president Walter L. Hervey,[2] "remembered my young friend." The writer of this letter of recommendation was a neighbor, Mrs. A.L. Seward,[3] who knew Hervey and was a friend of the Hervey family. According to the Teachers College catalogue, the president was given the discretion to award scholarships or tuition deferments.

Fayetteville, May 24th, 1892
Mr. Walter L. Hervey

Dear friend. I write to ask if you remember my young friend who desired to prepare for a Kindergarten teacher and also to know if she can have a scholarship this coming year. If so, I think the way may be open for her to go. She is a very successful teacher and the Board would like to retain her in the school here, so it will be necessary for her to decide soon. There are other matters she would like to inquire about. Will you write addressing
  Miss Carrie L. Pratt
  Fayetteville
  Onondaga Co. N.Y.

Kind remembrances to 'Mr. & Mrs. Hervey'
Sincerely, A.L. Seward

Acting-President Hervey must have replied the next day, because Caroline references his letter of May 25 in her acceptance letter:

June 4, 1892

My dear sir,-

Your letter of May 25 was received by Mrs. Seward. Please accept my sincere thanks for the offer of the scholarship. I have about made up my mind to accept it and will let you know as you desired within a couple of weeks. In the meantime, I would be obliged if you would send me a catalogue or give me information regarding the College.

Very truly yours,
Carrie L. Pratt.

Again, Acting-President Hervey seemed to waste no time in filling Carrie's request for information because she replied with more questions just five days later.

June 9
Mr. Walter L. Hervey
President of NY College for Training of Teachers
9 University Place

My dear sir,
The circulars have been received for which please accept thanks.
There are several questions which I would like to ask further:-
Last year I understood from you that my expenses would not exceed three hundred and sixty dollars. The circular informs me that they will amount to about four hundred and twenty five dollars. Did I misunderstand or is there a change this year!
I also understood that I might enter without examinations but that you would reserve the right of granting me a certificate. I did not think that you meant there would be no chance of my receiving a certificate, however. Should rather feel that I was working for something. Will you kindly explain about that!
Would there be any chance of my being in the college building or would it be necessary for me to board outside? Should much prefer the former if not more expensive?

Hoping to hear soon,

Very truly yours, Carrie L. Pratt.

Besides the fact that it is interesting that a potential student could have such immediate contact with the acting president of the college, another element of interest in these letters is the way in which they reflect the direct nature of the personality that has been ascribed to Caroline. They are consistent with the way she presented herself in her autobiography as well.

According to the 1892 Teachers College Circular of Information, tuition in the first years was $85 annually, which was not considered inexpensive at the time.[4] There was also an incidental fee of $10, a textbook fee of $10, and a matriculation fee of $5. Room, board, and laundry were $316 for students in the dormitory, bringing the total expenses for the year to $426. (Acting-president Hervey's letter reflected the same amount as the catalogue reported.) Rent for outside lodging was listed as between $6 and $10 weekly without laundry. It was not known what Caroline's living arrangements were, but even if she wasn't one of the 25 girls who lived in the dormitory, these amounts provide an idea of living expenses at the time. It was estimated by a former biographer that she earned under $300 per year teaching in Fayetteville because she did not have a certificate. Since her father's death, the family resources may have been somewhat compromised, so a scholarship seemed essential in order for her to enroll. It is not surprising that her correspondence included questions about the cost of studying at Teachers College.

This professional college[5] for teachers that caught Caroline's interest had recently been established in New York City. It originated in what might seem to be an unlikely relationship between the Industrial Education Association and Columbia College (now Columbia University). Named the New York College for the Training of Teachers, it began in the fall of 1887 and received its provisional charter from the State of New York in 1889. Although it did become associated with Columbia University in 1893, initial attempts at establishing a program for the study of education and teacher training were rejected by the Columbia Trustees. Part of the rationale was that it would mean that women would be enrolling, "a departure from the fixed policy of the Board."[6]

The Trustees were opposed to enrolling women, but the president of Columbia College, Frederick A. P. Barnard, had long held an interest in the scientific study of education, even though teaching was largely a female field. He influenced one of his students, Nicholas Murray Butler, to also study education. Butler earned his academic degrees at Columbia College, studied for a year in Europe, and then returned to Columbia as a member of the philosophy department.[7] Unfortunately, the intense interest generated by four public lectures in education which Butler gave at Columbia in 1886 did not sway the Columbia Trustees to change their position on forming a department of education. Butler and Barnard then decided that they had to start a teachers college outside of Columbia. Butler's election as president of the Industrial Education Association helped their plan to materialize. The Industrial Education Association was an organization dedicated to training teachers in the industrial arts and to creating a public interest in manual training as an intellectual discipline, which included the dissemination of publications on that topic. With the Association's support, the New York College for the Training of Teachers was established in 1887.

Education in manual training and the preparation of industrial arts teachers was the primary aim of the Association; however, Butler advocated for the training of teachers for all of their work at all levels. In the end, the College's stated purpose, found in the charter, was "to give instruction in the history, philosophy and science of education, psychology, in the science and art of teaching, and also in manual training and the methods of teaching the various subjects included under that head."[8] This broader purpose would enable the College to meet an increasing need for specialized training of teachers. School enrollments were rapidly increasing at all levels due to the recognition of the importance of education in the United States' rapidly industrializing society. Butler and Barnard's educational vision also had the effect of advancing the status of women by further professionalizing jobs that were traditionally considered women's work.

The College began with five teachers, one each, in these departments: history and institutes of education; mechanical drawing and woodworking; domestic economy; kindergarten methods; and industrial art. The departments of natural science and methods of teaching were not staffed until the second year.[9]

In 1892 the College received its permanent charter from the Regents of the University of the State of New York, and its name was changed to Teachers College.[10] Again the College attempted to be incorporated into Columbia College, but the proposal was once more rejected. Columbia was on its way to becoming a university, and Teachers College was seen as a deterrent to that process. Additionally, such a move would "commit the university to a policy of coeducation which would be a mistake."[11] The fear that a teacher training program would negatively affect the status of the college and the strong bias against including women in the student body were strong messages about the place of women in society at the turn of the century. And this was New York City, probably the most cosmopolitan area of the country at the time.

Despite the strong stand of Columbia College, the two institutions were able to agree to an alliance, which was ratified in January of 1893. Among the provisions were that degrees would be conferred by Columbia College, that lectures provided by both institutions would be available to all students, and that Teachers College would retain its own administration and control of non-degree programs.

Until fall, 1894, Teachers College was housed in a building at 9 University Place, in Greenwich Village, affectionately known as "Old 9." In the 1890s, the area maintained its unique village identity because of its geographical isolation from the rest of New York. Set on a diagonal street grid that didn't match up with the through avenues along which New York expanded northward, it remained a quiet enclave for most of the last 50 years of the nineteenth century. Known as the American Ward (it was numerically the Ninth Ward of New York), it did not have the live-and-let-live reputation for which it later became famous. The name American Ward comes from the fact that it had the smallest proportion of foreign-born inhabitants of any of the city wards. In 1875 32% of the population were foreign born. "A sprinkling of French, Italians, the few Irish required for political purposes, a scattering of the tents of the children of Ham" was how the population was described in Caroline Ware's ethnographic study.[12] Therefore the American element set the tone, according to a *Harper's Magazine* writer in 1893, of the cleanliness, moral and physical, of the Village.[13] With a few exceptions the Village was populated by substantial, well-to-do Americans. This quarter was considered to be a liberal lesson in cleanliness, good citizenship, and self-respect.[14] Such were the educational and social environments into which Caroline came for her first formal training as a teacher.

I was in my 20s when I began to look for the child's lost desire to learn.
It seemed to me that if we could keep this desire alive
through childhood and into adult life,
we would release a force more precious and powerful for good
than any physical force the scientists ever discovered for mankind's use.[15]

The 1892 Circular of Information specified that Teachers College was not a Normal School, because elements of a secondary education were not taught. There was a distinct professional emphasis: "Teaching is a profession for which a careful preparation is necessary." Caroline wrote with pride in her autobiography that studying at Teachers College was considered "an advanced thing to do...and we were a proud group of females from all over the country, bent on taking the newest thought back with us to the classrooms of our home towns." She described her classmates as "big-boned Westerners, and decorous New Englanders, and up-State (sic) country girls like myself."[16]

She was 25 years old when she entered college, and along with 125 other young women, she embarked on a two year course of study in the fall of 1892 that included an extensive list of courses:

Psychology

History and Principles of Education (a course in which she reported that she was an "unhappy failure")[17]

Methods of Teaching

Observation and Practice in a school for observation and practice

School Organization and administration in the U.S., England, France, and Germany

Natural Science

Manual Training courses that included form study and drawing, domestic economy, woodworking, and mechanical drawing

Theory and Practice in Kindergarten

The school year began on September 19. There were few vacation days: only November 8 for Election Day and November 24 for Thanksgiving until the two week Christmas holidays (sic) from December 16-31. There were three holidays in the second term, February 22 for George Washington's birthday, March 31 for Good

Friday, and May 30 for Decoration Day. Commencement was on June 8. The calendar for her second year included the same format of holidays.

I think the first time I questioned seriously
our accepted method of teaching children
was one day in our Kindergarten course at Teachers College... [18]

Caroline's plans to study to be a kindergartner[19] were short-lived. She soon openly questioned the Froebelian training methods to which she was being subjected.

> ...the more I learned of the newest kindergarten methods of the day, the more uncertain I became. Little children, we were taught, should begin the school day by sitting quietly in a circle. They could sing or have a story read, but the sitting in a circle was the important thing. This would give them an awareness of the unity of human life. There was a good deal of this mystical fol-de-rol, and to my practical mind it was more like learning to walk a tight-rope than to teach any children I had ever met. It had a practical value, as I have since come to understand, though not one with which I could have the slightest sympathy. You taught children to dance like butterflies, when you knew they would much rather roar like lions, because lions are hard to discipline and butterflies aren't. All activity in the Kindergarten must be quiet, unexciting. All of it was designed to prepare the children for the long years of discipline ahead. Kindergarten got them ready to be bamboozled by first grade.[20]

This story about dancing like butterflies has become the quintessential example of her individualistic ideas about teaching young children. It appears in a number of articles about her and was retold by Caroline in interviews. It also appeared in newspaper obituaries after her death.

Criticism of the mystical symbolism of Froebel's kindergarten practices was echoed by John Dewey and his daughter Evelyn Dewey, writing later on in 1915. They observed that in contrast to the progressive schools they visited, the traditional Froebelian kindergartens considered the educative value of play to be a demonstration of the symbolism of the laws of universal being. They wrote that according to these traditional practices "children should gather...in a circle, not because a circular grouping is convenient for social and practical purposes, but because the circle is a symbol of infinity which will tend to evoke the infinite latent in the child's soul."[21]

In her autobiography Caroline reported that this period was her rebellious twenties. She wrote, "My first act of rebellion was to go to the Dean and announce that kindergarten was not for me. Guessing rightly that country living had given me a capable pair of hands, he suggested Arts and Crafts. Soon I was happily hammering and sawing in the Manual Training Shop."[22] Nevertheless, she soon came to question the methods of teaching manual training that she was being taught and complained that while many skills were being developed, the curriculum never called for making anything real. She felt that children would not benefit from the kind of curriculum that did not include making something tangible and useful. This idea remained with her and was to become an important principle in the curriculum she devised when she began the Play School 20 years later.

Throughout her two years at Teachers College, she received her best grades in manual training courses and graduated with a respectable academic record. But she always maintained that children themselves were the source of her education, not teacher training courses or professors of pedagogy. She had little use for what she saw as the domination of education by "bookworshipping universities"[23] and their impractical methods.

After earning her two-year certificate from the manual training program, called at the time a Bachelor of Pedagogy, she was hired to teach manual training to future teachers at the Philadelphia Normal School in September 1894. She was now 27 years old.

Her experiences at Teachers College are significant to understanding Pratt as a feminist and as a progressive educator. Feminist thought during this period of Pratt's professional development included advocating for women's individual choices and opposing the self-abnegation historically expected of women.[24] While she did not invoke feminist ideology to defend her thinking, Pratt clearly did not feel that she had to rely on the word of college teacher experts to determine how she should think about pedagogy. Further, she did not quietly accept the educational ideas set out in the kindergarten curriculum or look to herself as the problem in their acceptance. Rather she saw the situation as one in which she could exercise her own agency. Personal freedom was more important than abiding by the social conventions prescribed for women.

In this formal teacher training, both as kindergartner and as manual training specialist, she encountered practices she could not accept. She saw them as being not only disconnected from the experience of the student but also unrelated to the reality of the task to ultimately be accomplished in the world outside of the classroom. Opposition to both of these conditions was embodied in principles of progressive education. An experiential child-centered curriculum, in which children learn from doing real work, is central to progressive philosophy.

The pragmatism of the progressive philosophy is also evident in her thinking. She had taught successfully for five years before coming to New York City using observations of her students and their interests to guide her teaching, and when "experts" did not tell her anything that she could use, it further intensified her pragmatic thinking about teaching. The idea that she could use her own abilities to teach, to observe children, to see what they did and what they wanted to do was strengthened during her unsatisfying time as a student. The power of lived experience took on great personal significance and continued to be a hallmark of her philosophy of teaching and learning.

Notes

1. ILFC, 11.
2. Hervey was named president in 1893 and served until 1897 during which time he worked to enhance the formal alliance between Columbia College and Teachers College begun in 1893.
3. Because the original letter is not currently accessible from the Milbank Memorial Library at Teachers College, the identity of Mrs. Seward cannot be ascertained. It is possible that she was Lucy Seward Noble, a neighbor of the Pratt's. Lucy married a banker and lived in Detroit. She summered in Fayetteville, was a world traveler, and moved in a social circle that could have included Hervey. (Barbara S. Rivette, Manlius Town Historian, personal correspondence, April 7, 2003.)
4. Cremin, et al. *A History of Teachers College*, 120.
5. Professional is used to distinguish the institution from the Normal School, which was the typical site of teacher training at this time.
6. Cremin, et al. *A History of Teachers College*, 21.
7. *Encyclopedia Britannica*, 1911, Vol. 4, 885.

8. Cremin, et al., *History of Teachers College*, 22.
9. Hervey, "Historical Sketch of Teachers College from Its Foundation to 1897," 19.
10. Cremin, et al., *A History of Teachers College*, 25.
11. Ibid., 30.
12. Ware, *Greenwich Village, 1920-1930*.
13. T. Janvier, *Harper's Magazine*, 87 (1893), cited in Ware, *Greenwich Village, 1920-1930*.
14. Ibid., 11.
15. ILFC, 6.
16. Ibid., 11.
17. Ibid., 7.
18. Ibid., 10.
19. This term was used at the time to identify kindergarten teachers. Nowadays it refers to a student in kindergarten.
20. ILFC, 11.
21 Dewey and Dewey, *Schools of Tomorrow*, 105.
22. ILFC, 11.
23. CP, "Learning by Experience," 71.
24. Cott, *The Grounding of Modern Feminism*, 6.

CHAPTER FOUR

Living and Learning in Philadelphia

It was here, truthfully,
that my education really began.[1]

THE PHILADELPHIA NORMAL SCHOOL FOR GIRLS had initiated its manual training program only six months before Caroline began teaching in the fall of 1894. It was the perspective of the school administration that even though schools employed specialists in manual training, classroom teachers needed to understand the value of manual training in the curriculum and how it could be related to other school subjects. Caroline became a special instructor in woodworking, training teachers to be proficient in skills such as gauging, squaring, sawing, chiseling, planeing and boring, doweling and chamfering. Her annual salary was $1000.

After four months, she and another teacher hired at the same time received praise from the principal of the school: "Without delay these ladies entered upon their new duties and are demonstrating daily, by their excellent work, the wisdom of the choice of the [hiring] committee."[2] A letter that Caroline received many years later, recalled her as "A bit of light in a rather dark educational pattern...thank you...for being what you were to us in our years for searching for a bit of understanding."[3] Despite affirmations of her work such as these, Caroline expressed frustration with her teaching program. "...I taught with the depressing conviction that I was helping to perpetuate a system which had no real educational value. My students would in turn become teachers; they would go out to spread the system further. What I was doing was as unfair to them, I felt, as it would be later to the children they would teach."[4]

It is probable that Pratt spent so much time on her own professional development during her seven years in Philadelphia because she was dissatisfied with her teaching. Certainly, her visit to

Sweden during one of these summers was a direct outgrowth of her attempt to understand teaching and learning differently than she had been trained to understand it. She went to the "fountainhead at Naas"[5] to learn the Sloyd System, based on introducing "useful models" into the manual training work. The contact with teachers from many different countries was stimulating; but overall she was disappointed with the course because the "useful" articles she learned to make were essentially graduated exercises in skill such as she had learned at Teachers College. Her comment was that the articles (she named egg whippers, butter paddles and salad forks) that might be cherished by some able housewife would be of doubtful interest to a child in the shop.[6] She decried "the lack of ingenuity, initiative, and imagination in the method. The essence of industry was left out of manual training courses, for who shall deny that the essence of industry is to produce?"[7]

In her search for better ways to teach, she also attended "courses for teachers" at the University of Pennsylvania, where she was "fortunate enough to encounter the iconoclast"[8] Charles Hanford Henderson, a leading spokesman for the new progressive education. She was later to credit Henderson and his writing and lecturing on organic education with influencing her thinking about teaching.[9] Another professional development endeavor was a correspondence course from the University of Chicago to which she subscribed.

Caroline began to embrace the ideas of Progressive Education during this time, no doubt because she saw them as compatible with her own thinking about teaching and learning. One example was Henderson's idea that education was the process through which the social purpose of life is realized. To him, the realization of social purpose meant liberation, freedom of motion, choice of occupation, enlargement of opportunity, and absence of all restraint save that imposed by the equal good of the neighbor and the perfecting of the self.[10] These same ideas were becoming part of Caroline's educational credo, one that she was eager to implement on her own. Coincidentally, they were ideas that were compatible with what we now understand to be some aspects of feminist thinking, at the time unnamed as such.

Probably the most significant impetus to her professional and personal development was Caroline's meeting and subsequent life-long friendship with Helen Marot, a young woman two years her senior. Her association with Marot was an important influence on the direction of her life and gave a focus to her independent thinking. Marot was one of the founders (in 1897) of a small library in Philadelphia, the Library of Economic and Political Science, which was a haven for liberals and radicals. People who held a variety of extremist perspectives came there for the available materials as well as for the opportunities for discussion. Caroline related:

> I took to spending a good deal of time there myself. With my own adventures in learning ever on my mind, I saw there still another aspect of education. Listening to these people, many of them graybeards, as they argued and studied, I began to see education not as an end in itself, but as the first step in a progress which should continue during a lifetime.[11]

The idea of education as a lifelong undertaking for the individual and a force in molding a better world would become a consistent theme in all of her subsequent education endeavors. Coupled with a passion to understand the world of children and their ways of growing and learning, these ideas were central to her educational philosophy. The more she learned, the more clear it became to her that she needed to put her ideas into practice. She had learned that the essence of industry was to produce, and so she began to find a way to produce the kind of educational vision she was developing.

Helen Marot's library was a place where Caroline and other women could engage in self-development, in contrast to the practice of self-sacrifice, which was expected of so many women at the turn of the century. Even though many women (Caroline's mother and sister included) joined women's clubs during this period in order to enlarge their understanding of the world, what they learned did not change their life styles or their sense of the role of women in society.[12] The discussions at the library were of the kind that changed participants' ways of thinking and being in the world. Such a situation could be considered an outgrowth of women questioning the culture's traditional definitions of gender, an element of feminist practice.

In 1899 Helen Marot undertook an investigation of the custom tailoring trades in Philadelphia for the U.S. Industrial Commission. Caroline assisted her on a part-time basis. She recalled this work as making a strong impression on her:

> It was for me a bitter eye-opener, that experience. The work was done in the home, with no limit to the hours the people work and no check on working

conditions which were also living conditions, and which from both points of view were appalling. The contrast with educational practice as I knew it was painful. Helen and I often discussed the futility of trying to reform the school system, if after leaving school human beings had to earn their living under such conditions as these.[13]

The investigative work galvanized both of them to social activism and in 1901 they moved to New York City to continue their work, Caroline in education and Helen in labor organization.

Helen Marot

Helen Marot (1865-1940) has been described as "a social investigator, writer, and editor,"[14] and as a "feminist (who) did not seem to care a lick for money, clothes, or fast cars. Her world was that of art, ideas, and reform."[15] Lewis Mumford, who first met Marot when they worked together on the *Dial* magazine, characterized her appearance as "spare and slender as a Shaker chair." She was said to have worn "mannish" clothing, bookkeeper-style spectacles, and long auburn hair worn swept back over her ears into a bun.

Despite possessing a calm, even-tempered personality, she was a woman with a strong passion for social reform. "You see," she once told a reporter, "I'm not a liberal. I'm a radical. I'm always in sympathy with the strikers." She believed in a collective state. However, she stated she would "not work for a revolution from the view of what we've learned from the Russians. But in the long run, Russia's dictatorship may prove to have been beneficial. We haven't enough perspective on it..." "We can't get a real communist state until nobody is willing to exploit a fellow man."[16]

She was born into an affluent Quaker household, a daughter of Charles Henry Marot, a Philadelphia bookseller and publisher, and Hannah Marot. Helen's education took place in private Quaker schools and also at home with a tutor. A contradiction was found in her obituary which stated that she was educated in Philadelphia public schools and made no mention of her Quaker education. She was encouraged in her intellectual and moral pursuits by her father who told her at 14, "I want you to think for yourself, *not* the way I do."[17]

She began her career as a "studious librarian of pacifist tendency," but her labor investigations turned her into a "belligerent activist."[18]

In Philadelphia she investigated the custom tailoring trades for the U.S. Industrial Commission. This direct engagement with working class women and children was to shape her work for the rest of her life. In New York, she investigated child labor and also worked from 1906 to 1913 as the executive secretary of the Women's Trade Union League (WTUL) of New York. This was her most influential post. In this position, she also worked with the National Consumers League in gathering facts which persuaded the Supreme Court to uphold the constitutionality of a law limiting hours of women workers. She led the waist and dressmakers strike in 1909-1910. "Whatever she undertook," recalled her friend, Lewis Mumford, "She was always an insurgent."[19]

After 1913, she abruptly gave up participatory activism. Her resignation from the WTUL was partly a protest against the lack of working class women in leadership positions in the league. Becoming a full-time writer and editor, she remained devoted to the liberation of women and children from the tyranny of the industrial machine. Her job as editor of the socialist magazine *The Masses* ended in December 1917, when the publication was suppressed by the U.S. government for antiwar sentiments and advocacy. The following year, she joined the editorial staff of the *Dial*, helping to convert it to a radical journal of opinion.[20] Her name appeared on the masthead of the *Dial* in 1919 with those of John Dewey and Thorstein Veblen, under the title of "In Charge of the Reconstruction Program."[21] The *Dial* editorial board believed that by building on the momentum of change that had been created during the World War I effort, it was possible to re-examine and re-shape the institutions of the country into a more humane form. While this proved a somewhat naïve plan, there were some examples of success. The City and Country School founded by Caroline Pratt was cited as an example of "reconstructing" in education.

Marot published three books, beginning with *Creative Impulse in Industry*, which came out in 1918 and was subtitled *A Proposition for Educators*. She dedicated the work to Caroline Pratt "whose appreciation of educational factors in the play world of children, intensified for the author the significance of the growth processes in industrial and adult life." Sponsored by the Bureau of Educational Experiments, the book includes a report of an experiment Marot proposed that "would stimulate the impulses of youth for creative experience, which would give them an industrial experience where the motive of exploitation is absent and where the stimulus was the content which the production of wealth offers."[22] The experiment adapted some of the concepts of the jobs program of Caroline Pratt's school to an industrial setting in which young workers would be partners with adult workers. Marot used a toy-making enterprise as a model for her industrial experiment. She believed that it was incumbent upon educators to see that concepts of industry be taught that serve the creative abilities of youth in a context of collaboration. She felt that the present industrial system was designed to serve the profit motive and in doing so exploited the workers by robbing them of an opportunity to participate in the production process.

Her other books were *Labor Unions* and *Handbook of Labor Literature*. A manuscript she was working on when she died, *Oneself, an Assertion, and a Myth*, about her interest in psychology that was developed in her later years, was never published.

In November 1919, after the *Dial* was sold "[Helen] dropped the preoccupations of a lifetime, as if they were so many soiled garments."[23] She began her own study of psychology and anthropology in order to "seek a more fundamental insight into the human condition."[24] She had seen all the movements she had worked in and for, with almost religious zeal, go wrong, and she was determined to get to the bottom of this persistent injustice.

In 1934, at the age of 70, she and Caroline Pratt met the artist Jackson Pollock and his brother Sande. They were probably introduced by a mutual friend, the artist Thomas Hart Benton. Caroline gave the Pollock brothers jobs at City and Country School that winter, teaching art and performing custodial duties. The $5 weekly each earned kept them out of the Depression bread lines.

Marot became Jackson Pollock's confidante and friend until her death. She provided a sympathetic ear and practical advice about treatment and recovery from his mental illness and alcoholism. He would often come to Marot and Pratt's house in the early morning hours, wanting to talk. Marot seemed to be a maternal figure for Pollock, and their relationship helped Pollock overcome some of the emotional deprivation of his early childhood. Her sudden death touched off a long depression in him.[25]

Helen Marot had a generous spirit. Sophia Mumford said that she warmed quickly to strangers. According to others, she shunned publicity and personal credit for her work. Her unmarried status was seen differently by friends Rachel Scott and Lewis Mumford. Scott related that she believed that Helen felt that she had missed something by not marrying, and so she made up for it by mothering everybody. She was always briefing her friends on what to do. Mumford's theory was that her "spinsterly feminism was partly activated, I have reason to believe, by an unfortunate love affair."[26]

Caroline Pratt and Helen Marot lived together until Helen's sudden death from a heart attack on June 3, 1940, at age 75. They shared ideas, ideals, and friends.[27] Their relationship has been described variously as "close friend(s),"[28] "partner(s),"[29] "life long companions"[30] and as a women-committed relationship.[31]

Notes

1. ILFC, *xvi.*
2. Carlton, "Caroline Pratt: A Biography," 136.
3. An unidentified correspondent wrote to Caroline Pratt after *I Learn from Children* was published. Letter in CCSA.
4. ILFC, 13.
5. CP, *Experimental Practice in the City and Country School*, 12.
6. ILFC, 13.
7. Ibid.
8. Ibid., xvii.
9. CP letter to Lloyd Marcus, Nov. 20, 1947.
10. Henderson, *Education and the Larger Life*, 49.
11. ILFC, 14.
12. Sochen, *Movers and Shakers*, 5.
13. ILFC, 15.
14. James (ed.), *Notable American Women, Vol II*. This entry was written by Sol Cohen.
15. Mumford, *Sketches from Life*, 108.
16. *Martha's Vineyard Gazette*, July 30, 1937.
17. James, *Notable American Women*, 499.
18. Ibid.
19. Mumford, *Sketches from Life*.
20. Antler, *Lucy Sprague Mitchell: The Making of a Modern Woman*, 237, footnote 6.
21. An example of *The Dial* masthead (Vol 66:781) is shown in Wolfe, *Learning from the Past*, 307.
22. Marot, *Creative Impulse in Industry: A Proposition for Educators*, 111.
23. Mumford, *Sketches from Life*, 247.
24. Ibid.
25. Naifeh and Smith, *Jackson Pollock: An American Saga*.
26. Ibid., 847.
27. Antler, *Lucy Sprague Mitchell*, 237.

28. Beck, "Progressive Education and American Progressivism: Caroline Pratt," 134, and Wolfe, *Learning from the Past*, 307.
29. Naifeh and Smith, *Jackson Pollock*, 263.
30. Susan Semel, "The City and Country School: A Progressive Paradigm" in Semel and Sadovnik, eds. *Schools of Tomorrow, Schools of Today*, 124.
31. Sadovnik and Semel, eds. *Founding Mothers and Others: Women Educational Leaders in the Progressive Era*, 256. Women-committed women were those whose primary commitment in emotional and practical terms was to other women. The term lesbian was not yet in use. When Freud's ideas came into circulation deeming same sex relationships morbid, the lesbian label, defining abnormal sexuality, began to be applied. (Note: in the current historical debate on the nature of women's relationships, some researchers maintain a distinction between women-committed women and lesbians.) See also Patricia Ann Palmieri, *In Adamless Eden*, xv and 137.

Figure 5. Classroom, 1921.
Figure 6. Classroom block construction, 1921.

Figure 7. IIIs classroom.
Figure 8. Block constructions from two classrooms
from the 1924–25 school year.

CHAPTER FIVE

Greenwich Village:
A New Philosophical Home

*The time came when I went out to seek a way
to put my own ideas about learning into practice.*[1]

WHEN CAROLINE PRATT AND HELEN MAROT moved from Philadelphia to New York City in 1901, Greenwich Village was no longer the same place as the American Ward where Caroline attended Teachers College (described in Chapter Three). The demographics of the area had changed as the city's immigrant population continued to increase. Italian immigrants began to occupy the tenements that sprang up on the blocks to the south of Washington Square. By 1901 there were tenement accommodations for more than 5,000 families. The area formerly known for cleanliness, good citizenship, and self-respect looked more like a tenement city of the East Side than the middle class American Ward. In 1902 and 1903, two settlement houses were located in the center of the Village, to serve the Irish, African American, and Italian populations that had now changed the complexion of the area. As the tenements replaced owner-occupied homes, property values went down.

Fortunately, the decline of the Village was curbed by a combination of factors, one of which was a need for a residential area near to the center of the city. So even during the influx of immigrants and the development of industry near the waterfront, "a few residents of a new type—artists, journalists, professional people of small means, seeking attractive, convenient city dwellings at small rent"[2] found their way to the Village.

An associate of Caroline's reported in an interview that Caroline and Helen were attracted to the Village because the rents were cheap and people's actions there were consistent with their beliefs. Subsequently, several of their Philadelphia friends also moved to Greenwich Village, presumably also for the quality of the intellectual climate. Some of these women were suffragettes and had other views that were considered radical. June Sochen wrote that the Village contained a large group of practicing feminists as well as a community of people who were philosophically sympathetic toward freedom for women.[3]

Surprisingly, this avante garde community was not the Village that Caroline remembered seeing when she moved from Philadelphia. She claimed that the village *she* knew was the one that was populated by working class old Ninth Ward residents and immigrant families struggling to establish themselves in their new homeland. She did acknowledge, however, that she became acquainted with artists and other creative residents of the Village. "I came to know many artists and writers and to be eternally in their debt" for their support of the school. "Creative people, doing battle in their own lives against the set ways of the past, they were quick to recognize and value an approach to children which would cherish the child's innate creativeness instead of stifling it....they had a ready sympathy for the precious individuality of the child. And they were not afraid of anything new merely because it was new."[4]

After moving to Greenwich Village, Helen Marot was hired by the Association of Neighborhood Workers of New York City. Meanwhile, to earn her living, Caroline cobbled together three jobs teaching manual training, one in a small private school and two in settlement houses. The records of Hartley House, a social settlement on West 46th Street, one of the places in which she worked, show that Caroline was paid $750 for a series of 250 carpentry lessons.[5] If this was about a third of her total salary, it would place her at the top end of wage earners in Greenwich Village at the beginning of the twentieth century. However, since she had three jobs, it is unlikely that all of them paid this well.

Considering her developing social consciousness, it is not surprising that Caroline found employment in settlement houses. The settlement house movement in the United States saw education and social service as partners. The houses attempted to facilitate social action through meaningful learning in which learners were able to define their own needs. Learning was an empowering lifelong process for individuals. Additionally it was an agent to facilitate the healing of society's social, economic, and ethnic problems.[6] These ideals had been introduced to Caroline in Philadelphia and she embraced them. Significantly, in describing the three jobs in her autobiography, Caroline made a point of saying that all of them were structured so that she would have a free hand in the way she ran the manual training shops. The freedom to work as she chose with her students was a theme that would become even more central to her work in future years.

The two settlement houses and the private school provided Caroline with three different "learning laboratories" in which she could work on the many questions she had about the methods and materials needed to help children learn. In particular she was concerned with devising materials that would be both simple and flexible. They had to be able to be used by children for a variety of purposes as well as serving as models of simple constructions that children could make for themselves.

The methods she used with these three groups were compatible with the principles of the sloyd method that were described by Henderson and those that she had studied in Sweden[7] in that children participated voluntarily and chose their projects rather than following a set curriculum of learning skills. Her only rule was that students had to work, and if they didn't, they had to leave the shop. It took some time for this policy to catch on with the students, but she eventually was able to win over even the most resistant teenage boy who she described as being "an apprentice to the gangster profession."[8]

It was during this period of searching for ways to teach children effectively that Caroline reported her experience of observing a friend's child at play. Educational historians Lawrence Cremin and Robert Beck both interpret her account as being one that seemed to crystallize her thinking about play and the appropriate materials for children to use to gain knowledge about their environment. The object of her observation was a six-year-old boy who was engaged with a miniature railroad system that he was constructing with found materials,

> ...blocks, toys, odd paper boxes, and any material he could find. Some of it was obviously salvaged from the wastepaper basket. [With these materials] ...he was setting down his understanding of the way things worked, the relationships of facts to each other, the causes and effects, the purposes and functions. This was thinking, this was learning.[9]

This observation proved to be a turning point in her thinking about teaching and her role in the process. Rather than play being just a pastime for children, she saw that play activity could be an effective early childhood teaching method. This important realization prompted her to quit her teaching jobs and attempt to produce play materials that would be suitable for children to use. She wanted toys that wouldn't limit the children's thinking—what educators today would refer to as "open-ended materials." She wrote,

> I would make toys which could be used in dramatic play...play which would reproduce the children's experience with their own environment....I carefully kept the toys simple in construction so that they could be used as models if the children desired to make others along the same line.[10]

An article Caroline wrote, published in 1911, suggests that she demonstrated her toys at a Child Welfare Exhibit in New York and Chicago. The toys were to be seen as a departure from those that merely amuse children to those that stimulate children to action—hence the name "Do-Withs."[11]

However, she was not successful with her toy-making enterprise. Her brief acerbic comment encapsulates this failed venture: "Mr. Castleman and I worked together long enough to wish that we had never met, for the toys were a dismal failure."[12] Apparently the toys were not appealing enough to parents to warrant their purchase. According to one explanation, the toys were too "abstract."[13]

It was her better-known invention of the Unit Blocks which, although not a moneymaking proposition, was and continues to remain, extremely significant as a tool of children's learning. Generations of children have laid a foundation for formal learning in kindergarten in the block corner of the classroom.

Blocks had been used since Froebel's "invention" of the kindergarten in the late 1830s. But as kindergartners began to broaden their concept of kindergarten practice through the scientific study of children based on the observations of the growing field of psychology, the complex Froebelian block activities were seen as restrictive to children's development. The Unit Blocks Caroline devised are deceptively simple, but it is their simplicity that provides the versatility needed for children's expression of their experiences. She wanted her blocks to be tools for representing the experiences that children had, both inside and outside of the classroom.

A few years later, she would write in a Bureau of Educational Experiments report that in calling her materials "free" she referred to the idea that they were not designed for some special educational purpose suggested by an adult, but were central to child-directed life and purpose. They offer the greater opportunity for the child's experimentation.[14]

UNIT BLOCKS

Blocks remain simply pieces of wood
unless they are infused with information gleaned from experience.
A simple geometical shape could become any number of things to a child.[15]

Building blocks are universally recognized as one of the most valuable learning tools of early childhood. While they come in various forms, it is the Unit Blocks that Caroline Pratt designed and made for her Play School in 1913 that are found in almost every preschool and kindergarten. Their widespread use represents a legacy Miss Pratt would be proud of because she believed so strongly in the power of blocks to help children construct their knowledge. In an early writing, she stated that "we pin a large amount of faith to block building for younger children. The reason for this is that blocks are the most adaptable materials for their use that we can find."[16] The simple geometric shapes could become any number of things for a child depending on what experience he or she wanted to represent.

Miss Pratt had observed children playing with the large blocks that Patty Smith Hill had designed for the kindergarten at Teachers College. Hill's blocks were the first that went from the gridded table of Froebel's gift and occupation activities to the floor where their use could be expanded according to children's activity. Hill accomplished this by doubling the volume of each of Froebel's cubic gifts. Later on, she enlarged them even more, so that children could build structures that they could enter. Ultimately the design proved quite unwieldy for older kindergarten children and unsuitable for the youngest learners. The blocks were used for free play in Hill's kindergarten, not as part of her teaching program.

In contrast, Miss Pratt wanted her blocks to be an integral part of the curriculum, not just vehicles for free play. Her idea was that her blocks were play material that embodied physical activity and learning opportunities about shape, size, scale, community interdependence, and aesthetics. They possessed qualities of multiple usage, freedom from frustrating details, and ease in manipulation that were essential to the nature of good toys.[17]

These smooth maple building blocks are unique in their construction. The basic unit is 1 3/8 inches by 2 3/4 inches by 5 1/2 inches. Half units, double units, and quadruple units all carry the same proportion of 1:2:4. That is, the blocks are half as high as they are wide and twice as long as they are wide. The collection includes cylinders that conform in height to the units and curves of similar width and thickness. (See Appendix C.) The hardwood blocks are cut and sanded in precise measurement because Miss Pratt maintained that it is this kind of precision that develops the most desirable building habits. The blocks are gravity dependent and hefty enough for floor use. They lend themselves to symbolic play with the addition of scaled animal and people figures.[18]

Miss Pratt seemed impatient with those who questioned the use of blocks, but chalked it up to a lack of appreciation of children as growing individuals.[19] Her observations of children as they played with blocks demonstrated for her that block building provided the opportunity for children to learn about the relationships between experience as well as concepts about their environment. She felt that each experience a child has provides preparation for another and that each concept that is developed opens the door to another that is as interesting and as worthy of attention as the previous one.

While every reference to the use of blocks in the City and Country School (formerly the Play School) curriculum was laudatory, one teacher did have a somewhat jaded memory of blocks, probably from her days as a student teacher. She recalled her assignment one fall to prepare for the opening of school was to scrub all of the blocks "of which Jessie Stanton* must have had at least 2 1/2 million in that room!"[20]

*Miss Stanton was a long-time teacher at the City and Country School who often worked with student teachers.

The Experiment in Hartley House

I had envisioned a community of children who could in their own way,
through the child activity which we misguidedly called play,
reproduce this world and its functioning.[21]

In 1913 Caroline began to enact this vision during a two-month experiment with young children from which the Play School developed. She found Miss May Matthews, head of the Hartley House Settlement where she had worked, to be responsive to her plan for an unconventional teaching situation. The only problem was that Miss Matthews stipulated that the assembly room which would house the class needed to be picked up and all materials put away at the end of each session. While Caroline considered this stipulation to be disastrous to her plan, she was forced to agree, having no other option for space. She had wanted students to be able to work on the products of their play over extended periods. But she couldn't give up this two-month block of time. It was her opportunity to try out ideas that had been fomenting in her active mind.

Edna Smith, her friend from the Women's Trade Union League, provided the funds for the experiment. Caroline characterized Smith as "an eager advocate of the rights of children."[22] Smith's father was president of a large construction company that made machinery for projects such as the construction of the Panama Canal, and she proved to be a good source of financial as well as ideological support for Caroline's ideas.

Caroline collected materials and prepared an environment to fit her conceptualization of a setting in which children would be free to use the materials to construct their knowledge about the world. Her hand-made Unit Blocks, the Do-With toys she had designed and made, crayons, paper, and clay were arranged in such a way as to be inviting and accessible to the children. "I had planned my display like a salesman, thinking of everything I knew about my small customers."[23] After observing blocks being used as free time activities in Patty Smith Hill's kindergarten at Teachers College, Caroline felt that they should have a more central role in the curriculum and be incorporated into the teaching program. She wanted to take advantage of the motivation for learning the blocks seemed to generate among the children. She considered blocks as the most adaptable of all possible learning tools.[24]

Because she had such a short period of time in which to try out her ideas, she selected six five-year-old neighborhood children, known to her, who would be responsive enough to enable her to see the benefits of the ideas she wanted to try to demonstrate. She felt that she didn't have time to draw out reticent children or those "who already looked at the world with dulled eyes."[25]

Beginning with the first day, to Caroline's delight, the children found their own motivation to play with the available materials. However, when they got stuck in their play for lack of information, she would sit down with them and discuss the situation, or go outside for a look in the neighborhood to restimulate the children's play.

Her recollections of this first group of children were more about what they taught her than what they themselves had learned:

> With my heart filled with gratitude to them for justifying my faith, I was kept busy checking theory against practice. It was so clearly right that play was learning, that this voluntary, spontaneous play-work was far too valuable to be ignored as our schools ignored it, or relegated to spare free periods in the school day, or to the home where a child could work out such play schemes when parents were too busy or too wise to interfere.[26]

In addition to clarifying for herself the significance of play in the learning process, Caroline noted the children's learning about socialization, including cooperation, with little or no intervention on her part. She observed that in the course of the children's activity "quarrels flared and died, rarely needing arbitration."[27] The materials acted as regulators for the children's behavior. She concluded, "They were also showing me that children learn to work harmoniously with each other the more quickly and effectively if there is little or no adult interference."[28] She realized that too many teacher words could actually interfere with learning. These observations were important in shaping her thinking about the student-teacher relationship. She began to see teachers more as facilitators of children's learning than as directors of it.

The Play School Begins

The attempt in the Play School has been
to place children in an environment through which
by experiment with that environment
they may become self-educated.[29]

The two-month experiment in the Hartley House was all that Caroline needed to see that the kind of school she had envisioned was possible. In the fall of 1914, with additional funds from Edna Smith and some of her own resources, Caroline opened her school in a three room apartment in Greenwich Village at the corner of Fourth and Twelfth Streets. She recalled that it was done with "more hope than money,"[30] a situation she often found to be the case in future years of the school.

Edna Smith and Caroline Pratt taught the students and shared the apartment with Helen Marot. Six four- and five-year-olds were invited from the neighborhood to participate. Two girls and four boys from working class families, three of whom were immigrant families, were enrolled in the school. She wrote of going out into the neighborhood to look for children, a practice she followed even after the first year of the school.[31] The picture of her approaching families on the street was accurate according to the recollection of a member of the class of 1928. He related how in 1917, Miss Pratt spied him, his mother, and two siblings at a neighborhood restaurant and came over to their table to comment on what nice appearing children his mother had. Miss Pratt then proceeded to enthuse about the new school she had started and invited the children to attend. When his mother protested that she was an artist and didn't have the means to pay tuition to a private school, Miss Pratt offered free tuition to the family. In the following years, all the children attended her school, and none of them ever paid tuition.

A similar encounter yielded two more students and the school's first art teacher, William Zorach. He related in his autobiography, "When I was in Yosemite Valley, I met Caroline Pratt....She saw Dahlov (his daughter) riding on a burrow and said to me, 'I wish you'd bring her to our school. I'd love to have her.' Dahlov was still too young, but I took Tessim (his son)...and a year later Dahlov also.....In exchange for tuition I went to the school for a few a hours twice a week to watch and guide the children in art work."[32]

Miss Pratt remembered her first group of children "in fresh, sharp colors, through the years."[33] They represented the mix of residents found in this neighborhood who were of the "humbler professions." While understanding the importance of schooling, the parents of these children probably lacked involvement in their children's education. Emily was the daughter of the woman who cleaned the apartment house in which the rented rooms for the school were located. Her father was a chauffeur. Albert was the son of an Italian waiter and an Alsatian mother. Katie was the daughter of a German-born carpenter, able at age five to translate for her German speaking family members. Joey's father was an Irish fireman, and Douglas and John, whose parents were not immigrants and therefore considered Americans, were children of clerical workers. All the children came from working class families, but were not struggling with poverty as Miss Pratt had experienced it in her social investigation work in Philadelphia with Helen Marot.

The Play School embodied an individualistic, child-centered approach to education, which was characteristic of schools that had a progressive orientation. In addition to the development of the individual, there was a strong sense of development of community as the children worked together to represent their experiences through block play. In an article in *Progressive Education*, Miss Pratt presented her views on community: "Children have to learn, then, how to get along with each other, first to attain their own ends and finally because there is a reward in having friendly relationships with one's peers or, on the other hand, in fighting what is disapproved."[34]

The curriculum was drawn from the environment that surrounded the children. For example, observations of a new building going up across the street, the bread deliveryman, or the children on the playground were incorporated into the children's play schemes with blocks, clay, or paint and paper. In addition to observations in the neighborhood, the children took trips to other parts of the city. The idea of field trips was unheard of in traditional educational practice at this time. In fact Miss Pratt may have been the first progressive educator to take children on trips to get them to study their world directly.[35] She explained her rationale as follows: "What I had in mind was to provide city children the kind of opportunity to learn through first hand observation what country children find in nature study....What I discovered was that this kind of study of familiar work activities fitted in with the children's spontaneous play interests and enriched their play in a way that nature study has rarely been able to do."[36] A favorite destination was the river.

> From our corner of Fourth and Twelfth Streets we could make our journeys, none so long as to tire young children; we could go out and find the answers to the children's questions...the six children and I spent a great deal of time at the docks. The river traffic, endlessly fascinating, brought good simple questions to their lips....[37]

The educational program for which Caroline Pratt had been preparing for the last 15 years was launched! Her activities during the 15 years that led up to and included the opening of the Play School continued to demonstrate the spirit of an independent, self-confident woman. She was an inventor. She developed both Unit Blocks and Do-With toys, and she became an entrepreneur in an attempt to market her inventions. She was an active member of the Women's Trade Union League, a group founded to organize women workers for the improvement of working conditions. She conceptualized and founded a school for young children with a curriculum that was definitely not to be found in other progressive schools at the time. These activities were not, in the early years of the twentieth century, included in the realm of women's typical endeavors. The work she did certainly was outside of the boundaries of proscribed gender roles at the time.

Even before the first year was over, Miss Pratt recalled that she began to think about expanding her program to two classes. Her co-teacher and benefactor, Edna Smith, was agreeable to her plans, and at the end of the first year, Pratt, Smith, and Helen Marot rented a house on Thirteenth Street to accommodate two classes of children. Edna Smith taught a new group of four- and five-year-olds and Miss Pratt led the original group, now mostly six-year-olds, to new adventures in learning.

To begin the Play School's second year, the two teachers again went out into the neighborhood looking for four-, five-, and now six-year-olds to enroll. Miss Pratt wrote, "Mothers regarded us with faint suspicion while we explained our program of play." She recalled that one mother supposed that there would be "a little religion thrown in." Miss Pratt observed that the mother had "accurately measured me as some kind of a zealot, but had made a mistake in my creed."[38] The woman did not enroll her son. However, during this second year, artists and writers did seek out the Play School for their children. This group of parents was more willing to take a chance on a new, unproved curriculum than were working class parents.

It wasn't long before others began to take notice of this nascent experimental enterprise in Greenwich Village. Evelyn Dewey visited the school in 1914 and included her observations of the play-based program in the book *Schools of Tomorrow*, edited with her father, John Dewey. This book described a number of schools in the United States that were implementing current progressive trends. The Play School was discussed in the chapter on the value of play in the curriculum. Miss Pratt remembered this visit as "our first recognition in the educational world."[39] Nearly as important as the professional recognition, it seemed, was the fact that Evelyn Dewey's visit generated other visitors, some of whom donated money after being impressed with what they saw. As time went on, it became increasingly important to Miss Pratt to spread her educational practices beyond the school community into the larger world of education. The establishment of her practices in public schools in the 1930s, which will be discussed in the following chapter, was a great source of pride for her.

One early visitor, who would play a very important role in the growth of the Play School, was Lucy Sprague Mitchell. Harriet Johnson, a visiting teacher[40] for the New York public schools with whom Caroline Pratt had worked at the Hartley House Settlement, brought Lucy Sprague Mitchell to meet Miss Pratt in November 1913, shortly after the Play School had its brief experimental session. Joyce Antler, Lucy Sprague Mitchell's biographer, described this meeting: "The two women were instantly taken with one another—Pratt forty-six, short, sturdy, somewhat mannishly dressed; Mitchell thirty-five, tall and elegant with her long bohemian skirt and colorful blouse, her crisp, polished, authoritative diction." Antler's statement, "It was this daughter of one of capitalism's favorite sons who would ultimately propel Pratt's theories about Socialist education into the progressive mainstream"[41] reflects her bias toward the importance of Lucy Sprague Mitchell's work. Those who worked with Miss Pratt would have countered that she didn't need anyone to propel her ideas into the mainstream. She was quite capable of doing that herself. Nevertheless, initially, she greatly appreciated Mitchell's enthusiasm and financial support.[42] She described it as "the beginning of a long and rich association."[43]

Mitchell's immediate interest in participating in the new experiment was reflected in her account of her meeting with Miss Pratt. "She was in the early stage of working out experimentally a curriculum of experience for little children. The idea literally thrilled me. Here it seemed to me was a God-given opportunity to work with children along the very lines I had come to believe were educational."[44]

It wasn't until two years later, however, in November 1915, that Mitchell presented a plan for her participation to Miss Pratt. She offered her services as a teacher; funds for the operation of the school; as well as a building, a converted garage behind her home on MacDougal Alley. This enabled the growing school to expand again which Miss Pratt welcomed. In the fall of 1916 the school moved to MacDougal Alley. Mitchell became a teacher, and her two oldest children were enrolled in the school.

In Miss Pratt's autobiographical writings about this period of her life, she doesn't question whether or not these are appropriate endeavors, nor does she wonder how others will receive them. Stories such as these, told years after they happened, tend to be structured to emphasize how the story creates or maintains an identity that is desired by the storyteller.[45] It is interesting that, while certainly unintentional, the identity that Caroline Pratt constructed to share with her readers is consistent with feminist thought and action of the early twentieth century. She could easily be seen as exemplifying one of the ideas of feminism that were cherished by the women of the Heterodoxy Club, the freedom to be "willful women, the most unruly and individualistic females you ever fell among."[46]

Miss Pratt was clear about the fact that it was impossible not to be aware of the ideas about progressive education that were being put forward and debated by academics, educators, and social reformers. Her enactment of progressive ideas was unique, however, as was that of other school founders in the first decades of the 1900s. Her emphasis on using play as a vehicle for learning is an example of progressive child-centered practice with her own twist, so to speak. She remained emphatic about the importance of learning from direct experiences as stated in an article published in *Progressive Education* in 1927:

> We are not willing to have the children dominated by subject matter. We want them to form strong habits of first-hand research and to use what they find; we want them to discover relationships in concrete matter, so that they will know they exist when they deal with abstract forms, and will have habits of putting them to use. ...Subject-matter of the past and the distant present contains fewer opportunities for these than does the environment of the children.[47]

The same theme is evident in a passage from her autobiography: "...the mere accumulation of information was not our purpose. We were not training for a Quiz Kids program—or its equivalent of that time or any time, the outpouring of streams of unrelated facts for the entertainment of adults."[48] Caroline did note that academics (particularly arithmetic) did creep into the play schemes of the children on a need to know basis. For example, playing store brought the need to count money and make change. "When we finished playing and had to count up the money to make sure none was lost, everyone enjoyed finding different ways of piling up various coins to equal a dollar."[49]

LUCY SPRAGUE MITCHELL

Both Caroline Pratt and Lucy Sprague Mitchell left individual legacies to the field of education of young children. However, for a time, during the early years of the Play School, the work of these two women intersected in a way that benefited them individually as well as advancing the development of the school. Ultimately, they parted and went on to be more well known for their individual work than the work they did together.

Lucy Sprague Mitchell was born in 1878 to a wealthy Chicago family. Her father was a partner in the largest wholesale grocery in the world. She was educated primarily by tutors before entering Radcliffe College in 1896. Her father did not support her desire to attend college. After college, she traveled and worked at a few different endeavors before she became the first woman dean of students at the University of California, Berkeley. She developed the position described as the "oversight of the interests of women," beginning in 1903 and continuing until 1911. After leaving UC

Berkeley, she went to New York to explore "...social conditions and the modern methods of tackling these conditions" under the mentorship of five prominent social activists. She wanted to understand the "modern woman," partially, her biographer, Joyce Antler, felt, to see how Mitchell, herself, might fit into such a role. Working with women students at Berkeley she had become aware of the dilemmas that educated women of this period faced once they completed their education and attempted to find their places in society. Mitchell identified with these dilemmas and postponed her own marriage to Wesley Mitchell until she was nearly 35. A prominent economist, Wesley Mitchell gave up his professorship at UC Berkeley to move to New York after their marriage because Lucy felt that she needed to be in New York to do her work in urban social reform.

After turning down several lucrative offers upon their return from an extended European honeymoon, Wesley took a position at Columbia University, where he remained until his retirement. Lucy was not settled professionally as quickly. Family values that needed to be accommodated in whatever she did were the virtue of work, the virtue of thrift, the virtue of accomplishment and the sense that you have to prove your right to live on the face of the earth by doing something for mankind.[50] Working in the area of education, it seemed, was the appropriate profession to meet her goals.

Mitchell was interested in children's language development and fostering it through stories with content that would relate to the life experiences of children. She wrote many of them for use in the classrooms. Some of them survive as Golden Books (formerly Bank Street Books).[51] Mitchell was also interested in children's understanding of geography, a subject that she thought was important to be presented to young children.

Pratt and Mitchell's professional work became even more intertwined with the establishment of the Bureau of Educational Experiments in 1916. The BEE was an organization designed to collect information about how children learned. There was a dearth of "scientific" information on educational development and Mitchell saw an opportunity to use the Bureau to collect the needed data. The Nursery School of the BEE, established for two- and three-year-olds who would "graduate" to the Play School at age four, became a laboratory for the BEE.

Caroline Pratt and Lucy Sprague Mitchell were two strong personalities who needed to have autonomy over their work. Ultimately professional differences arose between them. Both women had the same concept of progessive education, but how to enact it was the sticking point. Mitchell was more interested in the development of children through language (and stories) and Pratt was more interested in children's activity as the vehicle for development. While Mitchell acknowledged that Pratt was a "kind of genius," she found it difficult to work with her. "She was what one might call aggressively individualistic, too much so to be a genuine sharer. She had an intense, childlike even belligerent belief in her own thinking that made disciples rather than thinkers of those who worked with her....We could not question: we could only support. "[52] Miss Pratt was not in favor of all the records that Mitchell wanted to collect both on groups and individual children in the school. She felt that if the teachers weren't smart enough to see what the children were doing, then records wouldn't have any value either.

Mitchell began to believe that her own professional development was being stifled by her association with the City and Country School, and that it was probably a detriment to Caroline's development as well. So she asked Miss Pratt to begin to seek other sources of financial support. Mitchell stopped teaching at the school at the end of the 1928 school year and went on to other pursuits under the umbrella of the BEE, which ultimately became Bank Street College of Education. In 1929, she requested that the City and Country School take more responsibility for such school expenses as rent and utilities that she had been underwriting for the quarters that the school occupied on Twelfth Street after five years on MacDougal Alley.

Although the women had disagreements, it seemed that they maintained a professional respect for one another. Mitchell acknowledged that she had learned much in the years that she taught with Miss Pratt:

"I think I could not have learned as thoroughly or as rapidly with anyone except Caroline Pratt. But she clipped my wings. I think she could not help it. Caroline's way of thinking and working and my way of thinking and working were too different to make it profitable for us to work together any longer."[53]

Support from the Bureau of Educational Experiments (BEE)

After working virtually alone
I was all at once surrounded by what seemed like a throng
of eager explorers in the uncharted land of childhood.[54]

One proposal born of Lucy Sprague Mitchell's enthusiasm for progressive education turned out to be a mixed blessing for Caroline Pratt and the Play School. Funded by a generous grant from Lucy Sprague Mitchell's cousin, Elizabeth Sprague Coolidge, Mitchell conceptualized an organization that became known as the Bureau of Educational Experiments (BEE).[55] The purpose of the BEE was to document the developmental and learning processes of children. The organizers of the BEE felt that there was a need for accurate knowledge about the procedures of progressive schools to help teachers evaluate the abilities and needs of children as well as to review and revise curricula that were dictated by the needs of the children. The BEE began its work in May 1916, and incorporated in April 1917. Lucy Sprague Mitchell chaired the Working Council, the name given to the active members of the BEE, and Harriet Johnson and Caroline Pratt were members of the group.[56] The BEE was created to make an unbiased, scientific study of children's nature and growth. The information generated would be used to construct school environments responsive to children's needs. It was a goal to have the findings of the BEE implemented in public as well as private schools. Although financial support for the school was part of the benefit of being involved with the work of the BEE, the collaboration between the BEE and the Play School ultimately was seen by Caroline as too much of an intrusion into the activities of her school.

At the behest of the BEE, Harriet Johnson organized a nursery school for children from ages fifteen months to three years who would "graduate" to Caroline Pratt's Play School for children ages three to seven. These two schools became laboratories for much of the early work of the BEE. A unique feature of the BEE projects was that the observations of the children were done in a natural learning environment rather than a lab setting. Mitchell noted in the BEE 1925 annual report that "nowhere do we find studies of behavior which take place in an environment where children's activities are self-initiated and concerned with materials they can control."[57]

The BEE embarked on a very ambitious agenda of research in a broad range of educational concerns. For example, within the first month of the formal organization, the Working Council met to consider studies in industrial education, rural schools, the education of "borderline children" (quotes in original), precocious children,[58] and a plan to manufacture Do-With Toys and to consider the general question of educational toys.[59]

Establishing baseline data on developmental processes also involved an ambitious undertaking. The children at Harriet Johnson's preschool and at the Play School all received annual physicals, EKGs, chest X-rays, and analysis of urine and stool samples. These tests were overseen by Dr. Edith Lincoln, a physician hired by the BEE to serve the school on a part-time basis. Other BEE staff members were a psychologist, who did intelligence and other psychological testing; a social worker, who took social histories of all the children; and a health worker, who checked the children for hygiene and nutrition as well as monitoring the ventilation and temperature in the classrooms.

Early on, it seemed that sharing the vast amounts of data collected through the BEE projects with the teachers and staff of the Play School and implementing changes in school practices suggested by the data was a difficult process. There are multiple explanations for this situation. There is evidence in the many reports and minutes of meetings archived by the BEE that, while Miss Pratt was grateful for the support of the BEE in many respects, she needed to remain in control of what happened in her school. There was also evidence that the BEE probably had an overly ambitious plan of work and as a result, not everything they wanted to do was completed in a timely manner. Further, the structure of the organization seemed to inhibit the implementation of recommendations. The responsibilities of the various BEE committees seemed to be emergent and not always clear to the members. This could be attributed to the fact that the group often modified the organizational structure in an attempt to meet the growing demands for research.

The members of the BEE took seriously the responsibility they had to structure the work in such a way that the organization would be respected as well as would make a research-based contribution to educational reform. As a result, they were hesitant to release their data in any preliminary form, the consequence of which was that some of it never saw the light of day. It is also important to note that the original $50,000 of annual support that was pledged to the BEE soon turned out to be much less due to the vagaries of the U.S. economy, and some projects could not be completed because the budget wouldn't allow it.

A report written in 1918, *Work Accomplished and Work Proposed by the Psychological Department*, included the following findings about the Play School students:

> ...The function of this department was to ascertain not only what were the original reactions and original nature of the child, but also what was happening to him as a result of the regime in which he was living. In other words, the prime consideration was the child and his progress, or his appreciation of life, rather than any designated method of procedure. As a result of our study certain findings may be tentatively presented.
>
> **The Play School**
> The chief finding concerning the Play School children has been that they are a superior group of children....These children have shown a decided ability in constructive work. In those parts of the examination where the ability to put things together was required, they showed themselves superior to other groups of children.
>
> It is highly probable that in this respect they are even superior to those who had an equal original capacity. In other words the opportunity which they have had to experiment with in their environment has been the means of developing within themselves a resourcefulness and capacity not characteristic of children lacking this particular opportunity.
>
> In presenting a problem to the children of the Play School, it was noted that they were at no loss to understand what was expected of them....The school procedure has succeeded in equipping these children with a fund of information not possessed by the ordinary child. The experiences they have had in making their trips to the various places of interest, have given them a knowledge of practical affairs, which will be exceedingly valuable in their further life....
>
> The ability to meet a situation, and not only to handle themselves well in it, but also to solve the problems presented by it, is more characteristic of the children in this group than of other children....There is a freedom of expression called forth by the school regime, which will be a valuable possession in their future contacts.[60]

In the fall of 1919 the BEE funded the expansion of the Play School through subsidizing the next grade level, a class of eight-year-olds. This was part of a project called the Cooperative Elementary School Experiment. The VIIIs[61] class was underwritten for $3,360, including

$2,000 for the teacher and $860 toward specialists' salaries: science, music, shop, and animal study.[62] However, at the end of the school year the BEE was dissatisfied with the partnership, because the "steering committee" from the BEE, which was supposed to work with the class under the direction of Miss Pratt, was never formed. It was her position that the committee had not failed to function because of negligence, but that the teacher, who was new to the school, had not become sufficiently acquainted with school procedure to permit such a committee to function. The annual report stated that the "Bureau feels distinctly anxious to have a more intimate touch with the work of the two older classes which they will be financing next year. We hope to work out some method of cooperation which will not be too confusing to Miss Pratt and the teachers and still allow the Bureau to function more fully than it has last year."[63]

Nevertheless, the IXs class was additionally funded for the 1920-1921 school year. However, after one semester that funding (and presumably the funding for the VIIIs class) was also withdrawn. The annual report stated that the IXs class had been funded for the 1920-1921 winter semester even though the BEE no longer had any responsibility for the work. It was stated that because of the organization's diminishing income it was not possible to continue this financial gift to the school.

The Play School Is Expanded and Renamed

Support from the BEE enabled the Play School staff to expand their program outside of Greenwich Village. The reference to *Country* in the renaming of the Play School to the City and Country School came from a camp (also called a vacation farm) that was maintained at Hopewell Junction, near Poughkeepsie, New York, for a few years. The most complete description of the farm was found in a school information pamphlet from the 1921-1922 school year. "It contains a good sized stream, a hundred acres of woodland and pasture and fifty acres of tillable land....It is intended that this shall become a part of the school regime for older children. That is, they will spend eight months in the city school and two months in the country."[64] Miss Pratt believed that this experience was necessary for disadvantaged city children. She saw the lack of country experience as a serious omission in the children's lives. Interestingly, a former City and Country staff member had a different perception of the camp. She felt that the camp was an idiotically ambitious project. It was her view that the school staff wanted to have control of the children the year round so they would not be contaminated by the influence of others.[65]

Discussions about purchasing a farm were found in the BEE working council minutes beginning in early 1917. It appeared that several programs were in the works that could make use of the farm. The working council minutes of May 1917 recorded that in addition to a two-month extension of the Play School, there was an agriculture program for boys proposed by Helen Marot, and a school program proposed by BEE member Marietta Johnson, a progressive educator who was known for her organic ideas about education. In a later set of minutes, the possibility of purchasing a farm was changed into renting one and $2,000 was budgeted for such a project. In April 1918, annual report records indicate that the BEE contributed to existing experiments, one of which was the Summer Play School, which made possible the addition of two months on a farm to the school year of the Play School.

Possibly the paucity of references to the Hopewell Junction camp in school records can be related to the tragedy that occurred there. A child became ill at the camp and a local physician, as well as the child's parents, were summoned. Sadly, the child died and the parents blamed the school. According to Charlotte Winsor, Miss Pratt never recovered from that experience and, as a result, decided to give up the camp.[66] She considered it "an unaccomplished idea for which, with my strong feeling for the value of country experience, I still cherish regrets."[67]

The change from the name The Play School took place, according to one source, because Miss Pratt was having trouble getting parents to send their children to a school that seemed to be only about play. Another source indicated that Lucy Sprague Mitchell was instrumental in advocating for the name change. Finally, Miss Pratt recalled in her biography that the name of the school was changed in 1920 "Because the children resented it."[68] There was pressure by the students to change the name of the school because to them it was not a play school, but a school, and they were working hard at their schooling.[69]

By the end of its sixth year, Caroline Pratt's school had undergone three moves and a name change and was a thriving educational enterprise, affiliated with a growing BEE. A new group of youngsters, aged 5, was added each year both from the Nursery School and from new registrations, The current groups moved ahead to the next classroom. Chapter Six provides additional detailed information on Miss Pratt's radical philosophy, and Chapter Seven describes more fully the curriculum of the "mature" school.

Notes

1. ILFC, 15.
2. Ware, *Greenwich Village, 1920-1930*, 14.
3. Sochen, *Movers and Shakers: American Women Thinkers and Activists, 1900-1970*, 10.
4. ILFC , 41.
5. Wolfe, *Learning from the Past: Historical Voices in Early Childhood Education*, 311.
6. Crocco, Munro, and Weiler, *Pedagogies of Resistance: Women Educator Activists, 1880-1960*, 33.
7. Henderson, *Education and the Larger Life*, 148.
8. ILFC, 16.
9. Ibid.,19.
10. Ibid., 20.
11. C.P, "Toys: A Usurped Educational Field," *Survey*, 26.
12. ILFC, 20.
13. Caplan and Caplan, *The Power of Play*, 268.
14. CP, "The Play School, An Experiment in Education," Charlotte Winsor, ed., *Experimental Schools Revisited*, 29.
15. Winsor, "Blocks as a Material for Learning through Play," 4.
16. CP, *Experimental Practice in the City and Country School*, 8, 9.
17. Caplan and Caplan, *The Power of Play*.
18. Brosterman, *Inventing Kindergarten*.
19. CP, *Experimental Practice in the City and Country School*, 9.
20. CU, Lucy Sprague Mitchell Collection. According to a City and Country School publication (Hansen, 1990) that contained a chart of sample quantities of blocks used in the classrooms, the VI's classroom (to which the student may have referred since Ms. Stanton taught that age group) contained more than 2,000 blocks.
21. ILFC, 26
22. Ibid., 38.
23. Ibid., 30.
24. CP, *Experimental Practice*, 9.
25. ILFC, 29.
26. Ibid., 31.
27. Ibid.
28. Ibid., 37.
29. CP, *Before Books*, 3.

30. ILFC., 38.
31. Ibid.
32. Zorach, *Art Is My Life,* 73.
33. ILFC, 39.
34. CP, "Making Environment Meaningful," *Progressive Education* 4:1.
35. Caplan and Caplan, *The Power of Play*, 271.
36. Ibid.
37. ILFC, 42
38. Ibid., 48.
39. Ibid., 54.
40. The visiting teacher functioned much like today's school social worker. According to a description by Irwin and Marks (1928, p. 300), "the visiting teacher becomes a real agent of mental hygiene in the school" as she provided explanations to families of students' difficulties and established positive home/school relationships.
41. Antler, *Lucy Sprague Mitchell: The Making of a Modern Woman*, 239.
42. Ibid.
43. ILFC, 54.
44. Antler, *Lucy Sprague Mitchell*, quoted from Mitchell's unpublished autobiography, 239.
45. Conway, *When Memory Speaks*, 1988.
46. Schwarz, *Radical Feminists of Heterodoxy*, 4.
47. CP, "Making Environment Meaningful," 107.
48. ILFC, 42.
49. Ibid., 50.
50. CU, Transcription of taped interview with Barbara Biber, n.d.
51. Readers of my generation, who attended elementary school in the late 1940s/early 1950s may remember such books as *The Taxi that Hurried* and *The Pokey Little Puppy* with as much fondness as I do.
52. Antler, *Lucy Sprague Mitchell*, 245.
53. Mitchell, *Two Lives*, 413.
54. Ibid., 55.
55. The Bureau of Educational Experiments became Bank Street College of Education in 1950.
56. This group also included Mitchell's husband Wesley Mitchell; Elisabeth Irwin, founder of the Little Red Schoolhouse; Evelyn Dewey, co-author with her father, John Dewey, of *Schools of Tomorrow*; Psychologist Frederick Ellis; Harriet Forbes; Laura Garrett; Arthur Hulbert; Eleanor Johnson; and Jean Lee Hunt, secretary. MML, Teachers College Special Collections, Archives of the Bureau of Educational Experiments, May 26, 1917 minutes.
57. Ibid.
58. This study was proposed by Leta Hollingworth, an early researcher of the psychology of gifted and "exceptional children." She was a Heterodoxy member.
59. MML, Teachers College Special Collections, Bank Street Archives, Bureau of Educational Experiments, minutes of meetings on May 24 and June 2, 1916.
60. MML, Teachers College special collections, Bank Street Archives, RG2, Office of the President, subgroup 1, Lucy Sprague Mitchell, April 20, 1918.

61. The classes were referred to by the chronological ages of the students, expressed in Roman numerals, rather than the traditional use of grade 1, grade 2, etc. The VIIIs class is equivalent to third grade.

62. MML Teachers College Special Collection, Bank Street Archives, Bureau of Educational Experiments.

63. MML Teachers College Special Collections, Bank Street Archives, Record Group 2 BEE Annual report, 1919-1920, 4.

64. CCA, City and Country School brochure, n.d., 12-13.

65. CU, Lucy Sprague Mitchell Collection.

66. Hirsch, "Caroline Pratt and the City and Country School," 37.

67. ILFC, 60.

68. Ibid., 68.

69. Ibid., 9.

CHAPTER SIX

Defining and Enacting
a Radical Educational Philosophy

My own education was given me,
not in teacher training courses,
not by professors of pedagogy,
but by children themselves.[1]

THIS STATEMENT IS CHARACTERISTIC of Caroline Pratt's
iconoclastic thinking about education. She was staunchly pragmatic
in her views about children's learning, one of the qualities that led
writers such as Harold Rugg and Ann Schumacher to consider her as
a primary example of the radical progressive movement in education.
She was one of the "rebellious laymen"[2] who embraced progressive
educational thinking regarding the dynamic doctrines of growth,
activity, and initiative. Patricia Albjerg Graham, in her history of the
Progressive Education Association, considered Caroline Pratt one of
the "most outspoken advocates of progressivism in the New York
area" and "an extremist in curricular reform." Graham also referred
to her as the "principal of the highly individualistic City and Country
School."[3] Lucy Sprague Mitchell's biographer, Joyce Antler, identified
Caroline Pratt as a cultural and political radical who proposed a
revolution in education. "Behind Pratt's theory of education lay a
radical vision of a new social order to which the individual child,
taught to think properly, held the key."[4] These descriptors would not
be surprising to Pratt because she considered herself a radical
socialist.[5]

So convinced was Miss Pratt about the appropriateness of her
methods with young children that others described her as having an
almost religious zeal about her school. Her radical stance can be
demonstrated through an examination of her strong aversion to
specifying the nature of her philosophy, her unique enactment of
child-centered educational practices, her attention to issues about

gender equity, and her iconoclastic method of selecting and training her own teachers.

Aversion to a Stated Philosophy

Miss Pratt resisted having to articulate a philosophy of education. In an early bulletin of the Bureau of Educational Experiments, she stated that, "In discussing the Play School, I wish particularly to avoid the crystallization of any part of our practice or environment. There is nothing final about either."[6] She emphasized the consistency of her resistance to formalization of her ideas in this statement in her autobiography:

> All my life I have fought against formula. Once you have set down a formula, you are imprisoned by it as surely as the primitive tribesman is imprisoned by the witch doctor's magic circle. I would not be talked into marking out any blueprints for education, outside the school or within it.[7]

She didn't explain why she chose a witch doctor's magic circle as a metaphor for her feelings of being constrained by formula. But it certainly conveys a powerful image to the reader. She maintained that her resistance to a formal plan was both instinctive and desperate while intimating that part of the resistance might have been related to her inability to put her ideas into words. It is very possible that she did feel inadequate when expressing her beliefs in public. In an article about how social studies is enacted at the City and Country School, "Collective Formulations in Curriculum" (1925), she expressed great relief at not having to state the purpose of the school in the article, and instead could discuss the form through which social studies appears in the curriculum.[8] In fact, some of her friends claimed that she was inarticulate in describing her ideas, but she could show teachers what she wanted very effectively. "Miss Pratt could do with her hands, but she deplored words" was how one person described her.[9] In reviewing her published works, spanning a period of more than 30 years, it is clear that she consistently wrote in a descriptive mode about her views. She didn't make connections to existing theoretical frameworks or any explicit statement that she identified as theory.

Miss Pratt never denied that the City and Country School was progressive; what she objected to was to be put into a category of progressivism. She refused to be associated with any paternalistic doctrine of progressive education that was espoused by John Dewey, William Heard Kilpatrick, and others. Her refusal to attach herself to current progressive educational theory demonstrated the ideal that women should be free to make their own choices. Such a perspective was consistent with the thinking of Heterodoxy club members who were at the forefront of feminist thought and practice in the early part of the twentieth century. Heterodites believed that no artificial barrier should impede a woman's development.

While she would not write about her unique view of child learning, she did acknowledge some "outside" influence from the theories of other progressive educators in shaping her thinking. She wrote to Lloyd Marcus in 1947, the year before the above statement appeared in her autobiography that:

> So far as the school I founded is concerned, it certainly was influenced by American philosophers and educators. The Dewey School was started about '96 and Marietta Johnson's several years later. Both those good people were "on the air" constantly. Dewey published *Democracy and Education* in 1916 and later *School and Society*. Charles Henderson wrote and lectured on what he called Organic Education. As you knew there were others but with those I was most familiar.[10]

One wonders whether the fact that Miss Pratt does not make any explicit connections between the educators she mentioned and her own school was a purposeful omission in light of her statement above. It did enable Marcus to conclude that "her school developed experimentally along original lines, showing little or no conscious imitation of the work of earlier experimental schools."[11] Evidently, Marcus differentiated conscious imitation from influence.

Robert Beck brought up the issue of outside influences on her thinking when he interviewed Miss Pratt for his dissertation in January 1941. Comparing these two reports indicates that she had a different recollection in 1941 than she did in 1947! Beck wrote that Miss Pratt told him she did not evolve her ideas about education through play from the teachings of either John Dewey or William Heard Kilpatrick, nor did she know about the work of Colonel Parker at the Chicago Normal School's laboratory school. Beck thus described her as "having fundamental educational beliefs, but that she seemed to ride no hobby. It was not a school of Dewey or of Rousseau or of anyone else. Practice was altered as experience and imagination suggested the modification."[12]

In Maxine Hirsch's examination of Miss Pratt's writing, she reported that she found no evidence of a theory of education. She felt that all of Pratt's writing about her school was descriptive and was not connected to a theoretical framework. However, she did give Pratt credit for having an educational philosophy. Since Hirsch did not provide the reader with a definition of "theory" or "philosophy," it is difficult to accept or reject her claims about Miss Pratt's theoretical or philosophical positions.

Speculating on Miss Pratt's difficulty in explaining her ideas about the learning process she so passionately held is intriguing. Viewed from one perspective, it could be a manifestation of her strong anti-theoretical stance toward the "book-worshipping universities."[13] When she rebelled against the teaching methods she was subjected to during her early days at Teachers College, she set a pattern of resistance to theory-based learning that continued to be demonstrated in her reluctance to speak publicly about her ideas. Since universities were associated with theories of education and child development, her refusal to articulate a theory was yet another way of distancing herself from academe. The importance she placed on doing research in classrooms, based on direct observation of children, both with the BEE and with her own teachers, further attests to her distrust of the information about teaching and learning that came from universities.

She herself provided an alternative explanation. She claimed that one of the reasons she shied away from publicly discussing her ideas about education when she was challenged was that she had a fear of public speaking. "But my plea that I was too busy learning about children to make speeches about them was perfectly sincere. To spend my time talking when there was so much work to be done seemed to me wasteful."[14]

Some comments recorded by colleagues speak to the lack of confidence that she had about public speaking. For example, a letter Leila Stott wrote to Fola LaFollette in 1952 reported that Miss Pratt felt "enormous relief" over the success of her autobiography because it indicated that she had "really succeeded in being articulate about her ideas."[15] Once she felt successful, she no longer had any desire to continue to write.

Miss Pratt did try her hand at theorizing about her ideas, however, at least privately, because a handwritten and undated sheet of notes entitled *Theory of Education* exists in the City and Country School Archives. Whether they fall into a category of "theory" is debatable, but the heading is her own. The following points are listed:

- Children must have materials which they can work with, can dominate, can have in their power.
- Have companions of own age, on equal footing [they] can cope with.
- Teacher in background provide[s] each child with opportunity kept simple.
- Use materials which prompt the purposes of the child, which serve the present.
- Use materials so as to allow child the freedom of working with ingenuity, initiative, imagination.
- Child must be allowed to produce something useful and meaningful to themselves.
- The child mechanism works as a whole[.]
- Use adaptable materials which allow for their [development].

These points indicate how central the child's active role in the learning process was to her thinking.

Child-Centered Practices

One of the most unique features of her theory/philosophy was her belief that children's re-creation of experience through their play materials (particularly with blocks for younger children) was the best vehicle for their learning. While other progressive schools valued play, it was most often used as a free time activity. For Miss Pratt it was the center of the curriculum, the primary means through which children constructed knowledge. In one report she used an interesting analogy to describe her feeling of the importance of play:

> I am not at all sure that this interpretation of play is not a revolutionary step
> in education; it is newer in the educational process than structural iron work
> is in building. In the Play School we have not discovered the limitations to
> this kind of play—I doubt whether there are any.[16]

Play materials were so important that before each new object was introduced into the classrooms it was carefully evaluated for its ability to contribute to children's learning. This evaluation took place during teachers' meetings. Because of the importance that was placed on this task, there were many long sessions!

Harkening back to her rural New York State upbringing in formulating her ideas about the learning process, she was emphatic that all of the children's learning experiences had to be authentic. There were to be no make-work activities that resulted in a meaningless product. She saw such work as building a body of disconnected information, and there was no place at her school for such activity. She also stipulated that the activity needed to be meaningful for the student, not the teacher. She criticized Montessori materials on this ground. As an example, she pointed out that after a child had built the stair that was part of Montessori's didactic material, the teacher's purpose was fulfilled. The stair had no purpose for the child, however, because he or she could not use it for anything. It was useless to a child because it could not be stepped upon.[17]

The freedom of the child was high on the list of considerations for the teacher who engaged in child-centered practice. However, the freedom of each one had as its limit the freedom of others. According to Miss Pratt,

> freedom was good only it if meant freedom to do something positive and
> that something positive was determined by the child's interest in what he
> wanted to do. The freest child is the child who is most interested in what he
> is doing, and at whose hand are the materials for his work or play.[18]

The concept of freedom in a progressive school was noted by Fola LaFollette at a New Education conference in 1928. Examples she provided included freedom to draw up partially their own timetables and to allot time in a fixed program, freedom to select from several departments of the program, and freedom to take part in deliberations, resolutions elections, and sanctions. The notes end with an idea that bears a strong resemblance to Vygotsky's thinking about development: "The child develops through activity. This is equally true of mind, body, and character. His spontaneous activities, bringing him a natural satisfaction, accompanied by intrinsic interest, expressing themselves in play, have especial value for his development."[19]

The ability of children to be participants in a democratic society was an underlying principle that guided the forms Caroline Pratt's curriculum took over the years. The activities of individuals and of the classes had to serve a purpose to connect the students with one another and with the larger society. "It is the whole child we must nurture, not just one part of him. It takes a whole man or woman to live capably in our complex civilization."[20] The fact that she included "woman" in that statement is noteworthy. The statement could be an example of her shifting thinking about gender in that the first part of the quote uses "him" to stand for both sexes, while the second part includes woman as well as man.

According to Hirsch, Pratt's child-centered philosophy of education could be described as a belief in the importance of capitalizing on the child's natural desire to learn, by providing useful, real life experiences presented within the framework of play.[21] While this view is not incorrect, it leaves out the social purpose of education that was so important to Pratt, and neglects the social curriculum that was so carefully developed for children through the jobs program.

Gender Equity in the Curriculum

Did the school founded by a radical thinker such as Miss Pratt include what we now call gender equity in the curriculum framework? Was the curriculum what is now considered gender neutral? Her recollections of early experiences in the classroom indicated that she was aware of the gendered nature of children's play. However, she didn't seem to be taking any steps to change the status quo. The boys chose active play with vehicles while the girls "clung to their domestic interests….The only way to extend their horizon was by leading them to see the connection of the home with the outside world. Despite a few rebels, women's place in our society was still in the home."[22] As I learned more about her, it was impossible not to wonder whether she included herself in the above reference to "a few rebels."

Later, her discussion of this topic in *Experimental Practice in the City and Country School* (1924) is evidence that she had become more proactive about gendered play and the school was trying to counter the conventional gender stereotypes prevalent at the time:

> We make every effort to get all the children to play with these adaptable materials. (Note: She referred earlier to "materials which they can work with, which they can dominate, and feel their power over"). If the children come to us young enough, they work on floor schemes without much urging. The best work is done by the boys although there are good girl block builders as well. We should like to find out why girls are not so ready to organize on a broad basis as boys. Sometimes we may be informed that it is because of the biological difference in the sexes, but in the meantime, we are working upon the supposition that it is social. Whatever her future is to be, we can see no reason why it is not as valuable for a girl as for a boy to use materials which lead out into ever wider experiences instead of remaining centered in less active interests. In our own experience we find that we treat girls differently from boys. We cannot help ourselves. If we do it, we who are trying above all else not to make a distinction while the children are so young, how much more is the distinction made in casual contacts? Society cannot get used to "boyish" reactions in our girls, even very little ones. Excusable roughness in boys still remains questionable in girls. They are pigeonholed by the most tolerant of us, and by others they are victimized by deep-rooted habits of thought. Nevertheless, while we encourage both boys and girls with suitable materials to carry out domestic experiences, we also encourage girls as well as boys to follow any lead out into the bigger world. There are many references to this difference between boys and girls in our school records.[23]

There is also anecdotal evidence of the conscious awareness of gender in the work of the students. She reported:

> In all these activities (shop work and cooking and sewing), boys and girls were given equal opportunities, and generally their interest in one or the other was not markedly based on sex.[24]

She followed this statement with a story about how a holdout, a boy who was "stubbornly masculine," behaved when he refused to sew an apron, on the grounds that it was girls' work and he wanted none of it. He could not even be convinced by his peers. But when he saw the products of their work, which ironically were from the cooking class, he quickly produced an apron so that he could join them in cooking.

While she didn't declare herself a feminist, she was concerned about perpetuating both male and female gender stereotypes prevalent in the current thinking of her time. The idea that either sex should have to behave in a specified way was countered by her own behavior as well as that of other progressive women.

Training Teachers in Her Radical Philosophy

*It is the individual teacher who makes teaching an art as well as a science—
not the school principal, nor the school superintendent,
nor even the educational psychologist,
but the person who lives the hours of the school day
with the children themselves.*[25]

Miss Pratt acknowledged that training teachers for the school without a formal course of study created suffering for them as well as for her.[26] However, she felt that everyone had to construct his or her own knowledge about children's abilities to learn. She built her ideas about teaching and learning from her empirical observations of children and wanted her teachers to do the same. She wanted students to go directly to the children to learn about them, instead of learning about them vicariously through textbooks. Lucy Sprague Mitchell recalled this quality of Pratt's in her autobiography, *Two Lives*, "...she learned much from her experiences and little from words. It was both her strength and weakness—it made her understand children and fail to understand adults."[27]

It was Miss Pratt's belief that "A background of interest in social work seemed to produce the best kind of teachers...(they had the) initiative, courage and warm human understanding, coupled with an instinct for seeking first hand experiences...."[28] She revealed that she tried to choose teachers and student teachers for their emotional and intellectual maturity. She was interested in their human qualities rather than the academic qualifications they may or may not possess. She provided the rationale for her perspective in her autobiography when she wrote:

And such a school as ours, in which she (the teacher) had a basic philosophy to guide her but no fixed schedule of study, not even a standard of accomplishment which her children must meet...in which, indeed, the individual child determined the course and rate of his own progress—such a school leaned all the more heavily on the resources which she as an individual could bring to the classroom.[29]

A teacher who had worked at the City and Country School made an observation that is consistent with the above statement. The teacher wrote:

She was more concerned with the personality of the individual and, his or her relationship with children. Her early teachers were dynamic, for the most part well read, full of social concerns, and interested in children having meaningful experiences in relationship to their studies.[30]

The perspective of another former teacher was that Miss Pratt favored those who had not had formal teacher training because she believed college-educated teachers could only work with books, not with the real world.

Viewed from a feminist perspective, this stance indicated that Miss Pratt valued the ability of her teachers to make decisions based on their own knowledge, acquired from observation and experience, over that of outside "experts." She was putting into practice the feminist ideal that women (most of the teachers were women) should be free to make their own choices.

Miss Pratt, along with some City and Country teachers, met weekly with the student teachers that she had selected. In her diary of 1934-35, she made several references to working with student teachers. Some of these sessions were primarily geared to processing the observations and experiences that the students had written about their work in the classrooms. The following entries are illustrative:

March 20 At student teachers meeting asked each student how far they had progressed in write-up which I had asked them to do two weeks ago. No one had finished the article I had written on Imagination to them breaking it up and getting them to discuss it [sic].

April 3 Student teachers meeting discussed two write-ups which had been handed in by Miss R. on Wesley and part of Mr. S's on Jerry B.

April 17 In Student teacher's meeting we discussed two student teacher write-ups. From the standpoint of worthwhile discussion these write-ups yield almost more than anything else. The student teachers are eager to talk and the meetings begin to be more like round table discussions than a monologue as earlier in the year.

Other sessions were devoted to "thrash out our common principles and practice." Out of these, she reported that a unity of purpose and procedure developed. She used as an example, the discussion that centered around the meaning of the word "experience" in regard to the curriculum. Was a trip an experience? Is literature an emotional experience? Are some experiences more valuable than others?[31]

Whether these kinds of exchanges indicate, as well as the entry for January 2, below, that the student teaching experience was one of indoctrination rather than education (as did some of Miss Pratt's detractors) is left up to the reader's interpretation.

January 2, 1935 *Later I had the student teachers and gave them their appointments for the next month. I asked Miss F to wait and talked to her about her work which I told her had not encouraged me to feel that she is in the right place. I plainly said that she had failed up to date and that I felt she must take the responsibility if she wished to stay. That I was willing that she should go on if she felt she could come up to standards. She will make a decision and let me know. I sent her to get a detailed criticism from A. F.*

(On January 4 Miss F told Miss Pratt she had decided to stay after talking it over with her parents.)

The paradox that is evident in all of her discussions about teachers is that while she wanted them to be individuals who thought for themselves and did not follow any specific guidelines in their classrooms, there were definite parameters that she maintained for their behavior. These parameters were not always clear as evidenced by comments that were found in several sources. The gist of these comments was that Miss Pratt gave the teachers a free hand, but she came down hard on them when they deviated from her practices.

In the final analysis, Miss Pratt must have been effective in selecting and training teachers. There are numerous testimonials from former students which indicate it was the teachers who made the City and Country School such a special place for them.[32]

Notes

1. ILFC, 7.
2. Rugg and Schumacher, *The Child-Centered School: An Appraisal of the New Education*, 34.
3. Graham, *Progressive Education: From Arcady to Academe*, 44, 79, 88.
4. Antler, *Lucy Sprague Mitchell: The Making of a Modern Woman*, 236.
5. Ibid., 241.
6. CP, "The Play School," Bulletin #3, (Bureau of Educational Experiments), p. 2. This bulletin was reprinted in *Experimental Schools Revisited*, Charlotte Winsor, ed.
7. ILFC, 56.
8. This article was published in *Progressive Education* Magazine.
9. Hirsch, "Caroline Pratt and the City and Country School, 1914-1945," 69.
10. Marcus, "The Founding of American Private Progressive Schools." letter dated Nov. 20, 1947.
11. Ibid., 78.
12. Beck, "Progressive Education and American Progressivism: Caroline Pratt," 50.
13. CP, "Learning by Experience," 71.
14. ILFC, 56.
15. LC, La Follette Family Collection, Box E10, letter dated Jan. 27, 1952.
16. CP, "The Play School," Bulletin #3, 27.
17. CP, *Experimental Practice in the City and Country School*, 14. Progressive educators, in general, did not approve of Montessori's ideas because they felt the activities did not allow for children to construct their own knowledge. While appearing that the children were operating in a self-directed manner, in reality, the materials were highly structured in the way they could be utilized.
18. ILFC, 68.
19. Vygotsky, *Mind and Society*, 86.
20. Winsor, *Experimental Schools Revisited*, 48.
21. Hirsch, *Caroline Pratt and the City and Country School*, 76.
22. ILFC, 44.
23. CP, *Experimental Practice*, pp. 7, 8.
24. ILFC, 71.
25. Ibid., 60.
26. Ibid., 64.
27. Mitchell, *Two Lives*, 283.
28. ILFC, 62.
29. ILFC, 60.
30. Hirsh, "Caroline Pratt and the City and Country School," letter from Mary Card to Hirsch, Mar. 7, 1977.
31. ILFC, 62.
32. See Adler, *The Heretic Heart* and Edna K. Shapiro and Nancy Nager, "Remembering Schools: Recollections of Graduates of Early Progressive Schools." The testimonials of two former students interviewed by the author about their caring teachers are further examples of the high regard in which teachers were held.

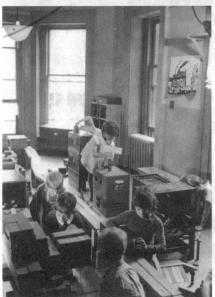

Figure 9. Amalgamated Bank construction, 1930s.
Figure 10. Classroom, 1936.
Figure 11. IVs class, 1940s.

Figure 12. Outside in the yard, 1939.
Figure 13. Building a bridge, 1944.

CHAPTER SEVEN

Education Practices at the City and Country School

But the school as I envisioned it had no fixed limits, no walls.
It would take shape under the children's own hands.
It would be as wide and high as their own world,
would grow as their horizons stretched.[1]

IN HIS AUTOBIOGRAPHY, WRITER LEWIS MUMFORD expressed frustration about his schooling, frustration that mirrored Caroline Pratt's experience as a student in Fayetteville. Mumford recalled that he felt like a prisoner, but he complied with the rigid structure so that he could escape as soon as the afternoon bell rang. If he didn't comply he would have been held there longer.[2]

It was not surprising, therefore, that he embraced the ideals of progressive schools that began in the early twentieth century. He was happy to have the opportunity to educate his children in progressive schools, his son, Geddes, at the City and Country School, and his daughter at another progressive school in New York.

What was it that Mumford and other parents found so appealing at the City and Country School? And why, since parents were so glowing in their praise for the school, did Miss Pratt have such a bad reputation about her interactions with parents? The answers to those questions shape the content of this chapter that describes in detail the City and Country School's curriculum framework, Miss Pratt's relationships with parents, and the manner in which the school was administered.

During the decade of the 1920s, the City and Country School's focus shifted somewhat—as did popular thinking about progressivism. The individualized instruction that was sought in turn-of-the-century progressivism to help teachers deal with students who came from different backgrounds and different levels of English speaking ability had morphed during the progressive "lull" of the 1920s into an emphasis on the expression of the individual.[3] This form of progressivism was less focused on social reform than progressive thought had been at the turn of the century. Rather, the emphasis was on conditions that would foster individual expression.

How much this change at the City and Country School was made as a response to the shift in progressive thought of the 1920s[4] and how much it was primarily the result of changing demographics in Greenwich Village is left to speculation and hindsight. It is not surprising that the expressionist influence would be strong in the City and Country School because of its location in the Village. The Village had begun to attract creative artists in all fields who were delighted to send their children to a school that emphasized the kind of individual expression that they were trying to accomplish with their own art.

Caroline Pratt's educational scheme was undoubtedly influenced by this aspect of progressivism. Her thinking also could have been shaped by her personal association with many members of the art, theatre, and literary community of Greenwich Village. Excerpts from early publications present her ideas:

> One of the contributions which I hope the Play School may make to education is in art expression....The failure to develop art impulse in education is partly due to the non-recognition of the fact that the free play of children *is* art....As the children play with drawing materials, with plasticine, with blocks and toys, with words, with dramatics, the emotions are freed and in a primitive way art is produced. The emotional processes in the children's play are identical with the processes we call art in adult life, and which, with an acquired technique, give us art production. It is what the modern school of artists in their simplified methods of expression try to realize.[5]

In order to foster art expression, the school was always staffed with specialist teachers of fine arts. The content varied depending on the teachers' particular skills. For example, sometimes sculpture was emphasized in the curriculum, at other times it was painting and drawing. Miss Pratt's recollection of the first art teacher, artist William Zorach, was enthusiastic, "especially because he refused to teach."[6] She approved of the fact that he provided encouragement and inspiration which was what the children needed. The City and Country School, like several of the other progressive schools in the area (Dalton, Walden, and Little Red Schoolhouse, for example), was very concerned with the development of art expression of their students.

Lawrence Cremin made an analogy between some of the primary exponents of expressionism and Caroline Pratt. He cited Isadora Duncan and Martha Graham as leaders in expressionist dance, Charles Ives in expressionist music, Alfred Stieglitz in expressionist photography, and William Zorach in expressionist sculpture along with Caroline Pratt in expressionist education.[7] The constructive activities of the children were expressions of their understanding of their experiences provided through the curriculum of the school. This focus was what appealed to parents such as Mumford and made them strong supporters of Miss Pratt and her school.

Even more important than the value of art expression for the students was Miss Pratt's dedication to the belief that "the desire to learn is one of the strongest of all human drives, and that the most important responsibility of educators is to nurture this drive in every constructive way imaginable."[8] This idea was paramount in shaping the curriculum. She elaborated this concept in a 1927 article in *Progressive Education*. It reads:

> To study the interests and abilities of the growing child as they are manifested, to supply an environment that, step by step, must meet the needs of his development, stimulate his activities, and orient him in his enlarging world, and that shall at the same time afford him effective experiences in social living – this in brief has been the thesis of the City and Country School and from it, through successive years of trial and error, we have built up the experimental practice of the school.[9]

This article was one in a series of retrospective articles about progressive education, *"The New Education Ten Years After."* Caroline Pratt's ideas about the place of experience in the learning process were uncannily prescient in respect to Vygotsky's formulations about the role of experience in the learning process. His theory, which he described as learning in the zone of proximal development,[10] was developed from observations of Russian peasant farm workers. She wrote:

> In order to have an experience, the opportunity must be appropriate. It would be beside the point to offer a boy a chance to sail a boat if he had never been in a sailboat. For a first experience he might go out with

someone; then he might be given the tiller, and finally he might help to manage the mainsail. All along he would be richly experiencing and developing. He would add to his store of knowledge about boats and wind and water. This would be an appropriate experience for any boy or girl of an age and disposition to take advantage of it.[11]

It is interesting to note that the practical learning experiences that took place in rural settings were important in shaping both Vygotsky's and Pratt's ideas about how children learned. John Dewey also cited his rural Vermont upbringing as being influential in developing his thinking about the role of experience in the learning process.

Curriculum Framework

...a school's greatest value must be to turn out human beings who could think effectively and work constructively, who could in time make a better world than this for living in.[12]

Caroline Pratt's publications about the curriculum and/or the activities of the school often carried the caveat that putting the ideas down on paper did not imply that they were to be considered etched in stone. Indeed, there are many references to the idea that the curriculum changed regularly. The expansion of the curriculum, including the implementation of the jobs program as each new age group was added, as well as the way reading and math were approached, are examples of the organic nature of the curriculum.

As described in Chapter Five[13] her curriculum was originally devised for younger children (groups III, IV, V, and VI[14]) and based on exploration of their environment through regular field trips. Returning to the classroom, the children were encouraged to express their experiences through play, especially block play. The block constructions occupied a large area of the classroom. The children worked on them for days as they processed their field trip experiences. Blocks were an example of the versatility she required of all educational materials used in the classrooms. Everything had to serve multiple functions, which limited materials. In addition to hundreds of unit blocks, classroom staples were paper, crayons, paint, and clay.

As the school expanded, adding a class each year, it was necessary to adapt the curriculum to the developmental needs of the successive groups. Miss Pratt saw the VIIs group as a year of transition. While still enjoying field trips and the related block play, this group seemed ready for some activity that would be more adult-like and result in a more permanent product. A combination of factors, including a teacher's perceptive observation and Miss Pratt's previous experience in teaching young children, provided the solution. A year-long project of constructing a model of New York City was devised. In contrast to block building projects that generally lasted for a week, this model was permanent for the length of the school year and served a variety of needs for this group of children, including a context for reading and mathematics instruction.

The jobs program. Curriculum in the classes for older children (groups VIII-XIII) revolved around practical jobs that each grade level performed for the good of the school. The jobs supported the goal of having a school that functioned as a self-sufficient community. Miss Pratt observed that "just as there is no necessity to manufacture jobs for children in the home, so there is none in the school. The things that *have to be done* are incident to any school"[italics in original].[15] The idea for jobs presented itself because the VIIIs were demonstrating by their behavior that they were ready for some "real work." Blocks had been the center of their curriculum since entering school, and they were frankly bored with block activities. They had grown beyond childhood make-believe and were ready to engage with the world outside of the classroom. The VIIIs teacher, who had come to the school with a background in retail, observed the children playing store. From this developed the idea to make the running of a school store the job for the VIIIs. The authenticity of this experience was enhanced because, according to Miss Pratt, the office staff was feeling increasingly burdened by this part of their duties and they willingly gave the job to the VIIIs.[16]

The jobs shaped the curriculum in each age group through investigations of questions related to performing them. The following description in a school bulletin shows the connection between the jobs and the social studies curriculum: "The (children's) interest in the materials sold in the store leads them to investigate their source of supply—an investigation which is further stimulated and augmented by trips and individual library and laboratory research. They study the spelling of words used in their own writings, as well as those used in store transactions."[17] These practices demonstrated Miss Pratt's strong belief that children did not learn according to adult-defined disciplines, such as history, arithmetic, or geography. The jobs program also shows how Miss Pratt practiced her credo of learning from children. While the description of the jobs makes the curriculum seem quite structured, evidence in her writing and in the records kept by her teachers indicated that the jobs program was refined regularly depending on the learning needs of each group and the questions they raised.

The IXs ran the post office. It began as an internal communication system with regular collection and delivery schedules between classrooms and offices. Later the job expanded to include selling U.S. Post Office products. Parcel post services were added when the school office asked for assistance in mailing requests they received for examples of school records. The store and post office jobs were switched between the two age groups as the school grew larger and the store became too difficult for the VIIIs to manage.

Miss Pratt reported that the store and post office enterprises

> occasion surprise in school circles. Bringing the children into contact with money seems to be too dangerous. We have watched the children with the idea that money may be contaminating at this point in their career. We have found nothing to verify our doubt....it seems to be the school's part to establish consumption habits as well as production ones. And how can this be done except through the early acknowledgement of many as a part of the present social institution? Children need to keep it in its place, not ignore it.[18]

The Xs produced all of the manuscript-printed materials for the reading program of the VIIs. This included vocabulary flash cards, reading charts and sentence strips. The job involved measuring and spacing in addition to producing high quality manuscript letters that would be used as models for the younger children. The task of supplying door cards for classrooms and offices was added to the manuscript printing job. This group also undertook supervision of the lunch room, serving as waiters and table cleaners.

The XIs ran the print shop, first using a foot press and, later, an electric press. They attended to all of the school's printed needs: attendance lists, library cards, stationery, the school newspaper, as well as Parents' Association publications. The students organized a craftsman's guild and established tests for apprentices, journeymen, and master printers that became a tradition in the school.

The XIIs worked on an automatic lathe to make toys to be used with the younger children's block play. At one point this enterprise was known as the "Never Bust Toy Company." Later, this group wrote *The Bookworms Digest*, in which they reviewed new children's books as well as "Old Favorites," a particularly popular column in the school newspaper.

The XIIIs jobs varied more than those described earlier. Initially the students made looms for weaving projects. Some years they did projects that provided permanent service to the school. For example, one year they redecorated the lunch area with a new paint job, curtains, and new tables that they constructed and decorated. A job that was popular for a number of years was photography. It provided a service to the school as well as an impetus to science study as students learned darkroom techniques, which led to physics and chemistry experiments. Some XIIIs groups served as school "handymen," especially during the years of World War II when carpenters and painters were not available. Leila Stott reported on this service in an article in *Progressive Education*. "On Miss Pratt's suggestion, our shop teacher organized a 'Do Your Own Repairs' squad among the older children on the general plan of universal voluntary service, and this has proved probably the most satisfactory form of war service we have yet discovered."[19]

As students performed jobs they learned basic academic skills as well as more sophisticated principles such as economics. Their jobs led them far afield into learning as they investigated such questions as How is paper made? What were the first stores in New York like? How did the Pony Express get started? What emerged from this model was a "community of independent young children who were actively engaged in their learning, while contributing to the life of their school community."[20] Miss Pratt's eloquent rationale for the jobs program follows:

> Jobs as the core of an elementary school curriculum have proved themselves to our satisfaction over and over again and from every point of view. The absorption of the children in their jobs, the way in which, like healthy plants, they throw roots out in every direction from the job to draw in ever more educational nourishment—in the practical skills, in geography and history, in literature and music and the arts—to us this is the surest

confirmation that we have enlisted that potent and precious force, the child's urge to learn, in his education.[21]

In addition to the development of the individual, it is clear that both block play and the jobs program fostered a strong sense of development of community. The younger children worked together to represent their experiences through block play. Constructions were often done with partners and remained standing for a full week as the children played in and out of one another's constructions. The jobs of the older children were designed to serve the school community as well as extending the students' academic and social learning. In an article in *Progressive Education*, Miss Pratt presented her views on community. This comment is included: "Children have to learn, then, how to get along with each other, first to attain their own ends and finally because there is a reward in having friendly relationships with one's peers or, on the other hand, in fighting what is disapproved."[22]

The Reading Question

> *...we were unwilling to make these [the three Rs]*
> *the center of the curriculum and to abandon the play program*
> *which up to this point was functioning so satisfactorily.*[23]

When and how to teach reading was an issue in early progressive schools, just as it continues to be in all elementary schools today. Parental desire for students to begin to read as soon as possible was a pressure that Miss Pratt had to deal with from the first year of her school. The ability to read was the hallmark of school success that working class and immigrant parents wanted for their children. Some of the children in the first group of students in 1914 transferred to public schools for first grade after their parents learned that the Play School would not be teaching reading to the upcoming class of VIs. The staff, however, observed that block building was still engaging the VIs, especially since it had become more collaborative as the children developed the ability for true cooperative play. However, when the children reached the VIIs class, they began to exert their own pressure to read. They were becoming conscious of the fact that their friends who attended other schools could read, and they were embarrassed because they couldn't. According to Miss Pratt, "social pressure of this kind probably determined our decisions that the Three Rs must definitely be taught at the age of seven."[24]

She explained many times that there is no biological age for learning to read. The age of six has been established by nothing more scientific than simple custom. To illustrate the arbitrariness of beginning reading when children entered first grade she related this anecdote: "I once asked John Dewey why six was the accepted age for beginning reading; his answer was that nobody knew what else to do with children after five!"[25]

Miss Pratt was passionate about the power of children's imagination in their learning. She was zealous about providing experiences for young children in which they could develop their imagination. But, in contrast to popular opinion, fairy tales were not the appropriate vehicle in her view. She believed that a child's imagination developed through direct experiences with the world around him/her. Consequently, she gave little value to the exposure to fantasy that fairy tale books provided. In fact she considered it counterproductive to the development of a child's imagination, claiming that fantasy provided superficial information that was not a useful foundation for the development of children's knowledge. Too much fantasy, she claimed, turned children into "premature little adults, carrying on a kind of intellectual clowning for the amusement of misguided grownups, wearing oversized intellectual clothes to cover a very confused little mind."[26] In her no-nonsense pragmatic thinking, she believed the better picture of a child was a "straight-thinking little citizen, with a good grip on reality."[27]

Fola LaFollette reflected the City and Country philosophy about reading instruction in a speech she gave in 1933. She stated that reading too many fairy tales was felt to be an especially unfortunate practice with children because habits of vicarious experience are established instead of the habit of firsthand experience. She further explained that because the world is complex for children, reality should first be firmly comprehended through direct experience.[28]

Miss Pratt's autobiography contains a related statement that expresses her passion that literacy not begin too soon:

> My entire life, and our school, and this very book have been devoted to the cause of demonstrating that education does not begin with books, but with life; that books are only a part of a child's learning, not even the most

important part. He will come to books in good time, but let him not lean on them too much, or too soon.[29]

The Mathematics Program

The cheerful feature is that no one is afraid of arithmetic.[30]

Like reading, mathematics was an organic part of the curriculum. It began with recognition of number groups of materials in the classes of the youngest children. The sense of number thus became well established before the children received instruction in written numbers at age seven when they began writing. The jobs of the VIII, IX, and X groups provided practical ways to extend their knowledge of mathematics. Multiplication, fractions, and measuring activities were necessary to perform the school jobs. An early description of the City and Country School program (1921-1922 school year), written for prospective enrollees, explained that while arithmetic was practical, students were drilled on basic math facts and operations, once they were established through experience, in order to facilitate ease of computation. It was stated that "they accept the drill cheerfully because they realize the necessity."[31]

The personal journal of Elsie Ripley Clapp corroborates the enthusiasm with which the students pursued mathematics. Writing about her year of teaching the XIIs group during the 1923-24 school year, she described how researching individual projects stimulated the students to ask for math work. "Finally the group demanded some mathematics. Their arithmetical information was far below the age-and-grade-level; however, addition, subtraction, division and multiplication when presented as number groupings interested them, and they mastered the principles of fractions and the methods of decimal notation with ease and enthusiasm."[32]

Writing later on in 1930, Miss Pratt acknowledged the consequences of the practically oriented mathematics instruction. She indicated that a characteristic of the XIs group that year was that they were anything but a unified arithmetic group, varying on tests between second and eighth grade levels. She expressed her lack of concern about this fact with the comment: "Arithmetic is unimportant except as it makes mathematics possible."[33] She was secure about the fact that when the children graduated to high schools it was with the mathematics skills necessary to be successful, having spent a great deal of time as XIIIs formalizing their learning to fit the expected parameters for entering high school students.

Monitoring Student/Class Progress

Was it not unreasonable to try to fit the school to the child, rather than...fitting the child to the school?[34]

The necessity of recording the activities of the school, not only to know what happened and why, but to be able to formulate a program that could be disseminated to other schools, was critical for Miss Pratt. If her ideas were to be implemented by public schools, accurate knowledge of the procedures and practices was essential. It was especially important since experimental schools were always under more scrutiny than public schools to demonstrate that children were learning, because of what were generally viewed as unorthodox educational practices. How to develop a method for recording consumed a great deal of her energy as well as that of the Bureau of Educational Experiments. Probably the idea of the BEE doing observations and record keeping was initially appealing to her, because it was a very time-consuming, labor-intensive process. Both group and individual records of the students needed to be kept, but at the outset of this endeavor Miss Pratt's attention was placed primarily on group records in order to have a plan that other schools could use.

Mary Marot (Helen Marot's sister and a former visiting teacher in New York) was hired by the BEE in 1918 for their record-keeping project. Her duty was "1) to devise a method of keeping records which shall help the teacher in her evaluation of [the children's] abilities and needs 2) [to organize] a scheme whereby the daily program and general curriculum shall be a matter of record which can be reviewed and revised as circumstances demand."[35]

For a time, both the BEE staff and the City and Country teachers were observing and recording student and class behaviors. This situation became a bone of contention between Miss Pratt and Lucy Sprague Mitchell and contributed to a deepening rift between them. Miss Pratt felt that too many records were being kept and that it had become a distraction for the teachers and students alike. Mrs. Mitchell's autobiography also documented this problem: "That is where we split with City and Country School. That was Caroline Pratt's school and she had no interest in records at all, not at all. She said that if you aren't smart enough to see what the child is doing, then your records won't do anything for you."[36] This difference in philosophy is what eventually caused the BEE, in 1928, to stop using the school for their study of children.

Lucy Sprague Mitchell's complaint was overstated, probably out of frustration with Pratt's seemingly rigid position about records. In fact, Miss Pratt felt that the recording of school activities and student behavior was very important. However, she wanted to implement her own ideas which she worked hard to establish. Because the curriculum was based on the interests of the children and therefore varied from year to year at each grade level, it was difficult to make sure the desired balance was maintained. In order to keep track of the elements of the curriculum, she devised a plan to categorize the work that each teacher used. The first two elements documented the core of the curriculum and the second two recorded what she called supplementary elements. What would be the core of the curriculum in most schools, the reading and math areas, are contained in the supplementary activities of Miss Pratt's curriculum organization.

- **Play Experiences**, including block building, dramatic play, and art which enable children to interpret their environment.
- **Practical Experiences**, including shop work, cooking, and care of materials which result in a product.
- **Skills or Techniques**, including sense training, number work, language arts, music techniques.
- **Enrichment of Experience** (later known as **Organization of Information**) including trips, discussions, use of books and stories, and all the ways of seeking and pooling information.[37]

Each teacher kept a narrative account of the classroom activities using the above categories as guides, as well as accounts of individual children's behavior. Using this organizational system facilitated the teachers' abilities to compare their classroom activities and skills with one another.

Miss Pratt was very pleased with what finally resulted. In January, 1932, she wrote the following to Fola LaFollette: "We are all working on 'write-ups' of children under my headings. This is my third year of them, and I am mighty hopeful that they are going to prove a real contribution to Education. I went away for a week between Xmas and New Years, taking the writeups of three consecutive years of four children and proved to myself at least that the job was worthwhile. If we succeed in this we shall certainly be the first to do so under such a regime as ours—or the first of the progressive schools to do so."

The following summer, in a July 23, 1933 letter written to Fola LaFollette from Martha's Vineyard, Pratt enthusiastically wrote again about the school records: "You will be interested in our individual records. We have four years of them now, written up under uniform headings and I think they show growth in individuals, though perhaps the <u>why</u> is not so clear as it might be (underline in original). To have these records is a god-send to me....I spend the summer bringing out the qualities indicated under headings integrating and un- or disintegrating. Or what we have to work with and what we have to work against."[38]

Parents: Uneasy Relationships

*I have been accused to my face of hating parents,
of wishing all children could be born orphans.*[39]

Parents were not protected from Miss Pratt's forthright manner of interaction. Some of her most pointed comments were directed to them and the quote above from her autobiography is a prime example. Her adversarial relationships with parents became legendary; even her obituary in the *New York Times* (June 7, 1954) mentioned that she trusted children but not their parents. She described her own paradoxical thinking about parents in this way, "So I have been of two minds about parents all my life, half the time wondering why they sometimes give so little of themselves to their children—and the other half of the time convinced that children would be better off without them altogether."[40]

This report of a parent by whom she was clearly underwhelmed illustrates the first part of the paradox she described, the "disconnected" parent:

A mother with very little staying power in her effort to do the right thing for them (her two sons). Her intentions are good but she is not the kind of person who you could expect to do any follow up work with the children or in fact put through any thought out policy. She is a charming personality, the kind to fascinate the male but not the person to bring up his children. This I got as much from what she said as I got from the husband.[41]

The second viewpoint, disdain for the over involved parent, can be illustrated by an entry in her 1934-35 diary on May 8. She wrote:

A Mrs. B came in to look over the school and possibly enter a five year old child. She was not interested in anything except whether or not the five and six year groups would be a place for her youngster and finally said she should consider it only for a year or two as the child would enter Brearley [a private school in New York] finally. I said we should not be willing to take her if that were the case and tried to explain what we were trying to do and probably antagonized her by saying that we considered ourselves professional in our occupation and expected parents to enter children with the expectation of cooperating with the school in what it was trying to do for them and a parent who was convinced that she knew best was not in a position to cooperate. She left quite outraged and said she would continue to decide what was best for her child.[42]

Another example of her frustration with over-involved parents can be found in a 1938 letter she began to a parent as follows: "Regarding our conversation yesterday, I am so positive that I am right in feeling that you should not have anything to do with A__'s work that I am going to put it down on paper."[43] This was a situation in which she felt that the mother was inhibiting her daughter's independence. This same parent, upon reading Miss Pratt's newly released autobiography ten years later, wrote to her, "To me reading it was a humbling experience. I could remember the times I would torment you with my anxiety of the children's schooling. Tho [sic] I had an enormous admiration of the school, I didn't understand your subtle, original, and deeply significant approach."[44] Miss Pratt must have felt very gratified to receive that response to her book.

In addition to the personalities and child-rearing practices of some of the parents, the unique nature of the City and Country School was also a deterrent to parent involvement. Most parents had experienced a very different kind of schooling when they were growing up, and they found it difficult to understand the nontraditional practices in City and Country classrooms. To make this point, Miss Pratt provided a picture of a traditional school (which many readers of this book may consider to be remarkably similar to what they currently find in their own classrooms—a consequence of the emphasis on narrow standards of achievement and high stakes testing). She wrote:

> Every progressive school offers a challenge to adults because in order to understand what is going on in it, the grown-up must forget all his own early schooling. He must forget that he depended upon the teacher to keep him straight. He must forget the pranks he played upon the teacher to square himself with her, the amazing tricks he played on the other children to get them into trouble and which they seized every opportunity to return when the teacher's attention was off. He must forget the very furnishings of the old school rooms with their monotonous rows of desks and blackboards. He must forget that it was a sin to look out of the window for a moment, to help one's friend to solve a problem, to walk across the room without permission, to whisper a remark into another's ear. He must forget about the old signals for folding hands in front or behind one, for rising in unison, signals which governed the whole class. He must forget that he had to march in long lines from classroom to classroom, that there were penalties for little faults and failures which left the teacher helpless and inadequate in the face of crime such as petty thefts. All these as a necessary part of a school he must get out of his system, for the new schools are not like this.[45]

Despite many stories reporting her difficulty with parental relationships, Miss Pratt didn't always project sternness. Diary entries and letters document exchanges with parents that revealed the quick wit attributed to her. A letter she received on March 5, 1924, contained this paragraph that showed a parent's appreciation of her sense of humor: "I do hope to see you soon and talk about Randall. I think he has made fine progress this year, but am considerably tempted to put him in an uptown school next year. I still have my old doubt as to how long we dare let a boy go on under the delusion that life is interesting and stimulating."

Miss Pratt's diary contained the following entry in November 1934: "(A p)arent came in to ask what to do because her four year old did not want to come to school. I said let her stay home and not make it very pleasant for her. She was much amused by this and went away laughing."

She made this pointed observation about the father/son relationship and baseball: there was "something like a magic circle that enclosed a father, his son and a World Series game, and I have never quite got my foot into the circle." She didn't object to baseball, but to children in crowds. She also had no use for the circus, because she felt that no child should be subjected to such a "monster of bigness...and when parents have had the effrontery to take their children out of school to subject them to such an experience, I have no compunction in venting my wrath on them."[46]

In her autobiography, Miss Pratt wrote that "the doors of the school were always open to them [parents], they were always welcome to sit in the classroom or stand in the yard [playground]...."[47] She was possibly recalling some of the earlier days in the City and Country School history, because a different story came from a teacher who taught during the last years of Miss Pratt's tenure as principal. This teacher recalled in a 1999 interview, "Parents were not welcome in the school. The teachers and Pratt ran the school. I think she was afraid of parents...she knew children, but not parents." Miss Pratt herself wrote about being afraid of parents, but for another reason. She explained: "for my own part I was afraid that they would get in our way, that they would attempt to curtail our freedom of action, try to steer us closer to the more familiar, more comfortable kind of school.[48]

Clearly, Miss Pratt's interactions with parents had a public as well as a private face. Publicly, her early writings indicate an indebtedness to parental support. In her 1924 publication *Experimental Practice in the City and Country School*, she wrote, "We have established ourselves finally through parents who were already interested in a new type of education for their children. Such parents are moving into our neighborhood each year in order to send their children to our school. That people were looking for such a school was evidenced by the number of families which moved into the neighborhood to take advantage of it."[49] Indeed several former students have talked about their families moving to Greenwich Village because of the City and Country School.

The parent newsletter, *Parents' Crier,* of March 1945, summarized the uneasy relationship that Miss Pratt had with parents in the following quote:

> Caroline Pratt has made the kind of school that children like. To all parents at one time or another, the sense of it has seemed to be a secret between her and the children. She has often been suspect as a traitor to the adult conspiracy. But parents who can wait for their children to grow according to the natural law, see them grow whole, in command of the full range and pitch of their energies, unafraid of their heart's desire.[50]

School Governance and Miss Pratt's Leadership Style

Miss Pratt was always addressed as "Miss Pratt" at school, even though all the other teachers and staff were called by their first names and frequently by nicknames. This was a clear example of her authority at City and Country School. She was definitely completely in charge of all aspects of the school. She believed that her authority came from the strength of her educational vision, her own intelligent ability to judge people and situations, and her understanding of what children need for growth. In her autobiography, she confessed to running the school "pretty much as I wished."[51] She explained that she felt that her role was to oversee the school as a whole and ensure the necessary flexibility for innovative practices to be implemented as they presented themselves.

Anyone in a leadership position is seen in a variety of ways by those who work in subordinate roles. There can never be total consensus because everyone interprets the leader's work from his or her own experience. So, this section can only present a range of interpretations of Caroline Pratt's leadership style that has been uncovered in archival searching. "Miss Pratt, though irascible, was an arresting personality," claimed Elsie Clapp, a comment that captured succinctly the range of responses to Caroline.[52]

Carlton described positive aspects of Miss Pratt's leadership style in the text of her dissertation. She wrote that Miss Pratt had a "dominant personality with great personal charm and a twinkling sense of humor," that she was a "wise and all-knowing person with an impeccable judgment of character," and that she was "helpful and supportive to teachers who sought her advice." Apparently Carlton didn't want to leave her readers with the idea that Pratt was a problematic leader because she glossed over her possible defects in this area, using a footnote to discuss less desirable attributes of her leadership:

> Some chose to see Caroline Pratt in a negative light. They interpreted her insistence on following her own vision of education, coupled with her supreme self-confidence in her own judgment, as revealing a dictatorial nature, inflexibility of thought, and intolerance for those who dared oppose her....If the severity of her judgment made her seem blunt and tactless, she was never intentionally mean or cruel nor meant to hurt others. On the whole, people seemed to appreciate her honesty because they always knew exactly where they stood with her.[53]

On the other hand, Susan Semel, who has written more recently about Caroline Pratt and the City and Country School, chose to describe Miss Pratt's leadership in a more direct way. According to Semel, one graduate…likened the way the school was run to "national Socialism in Russia." She further stated that, "When it came down to brass tacks, she [Pratt] made the decisions. She ran it like Stalin." Furthermore this source noted that although the executive committee was composed of teachers and parents who were "heavy duty guys who were very affluent," Pratt "would and did dominate these people." Executive committee meetings, it was said, took place in Miss Pratt's office, where the members enjoyed cocktails and hors d'oeuvres. Her "talent for management lay in the way she 'let the women drink martinis while convincing them that she had listened to and taken up their ideas.' Clearly," Semel concluded, "the vision of its founder [of a democratic learning environment] is at odds with the way in which she chose to implement it."[54]

A former student also failed to see evidence of a democratic environment in Miss Pratt's interactions with students. "We were all terrified of her. She was stern. If you were sent to the office she made you feel like sin incarnate. She did not spread the feeling of joy and warmth in the school that we got from all the other members of the staff." In retrospect, this student, as did Semel, understood Miss Pratt's severe behavior as a contradiction of liberal education practices.

Miss Pratt's position as the sole authority was supported by staff members who were trained at City and Country, whether or not they had previous educational experiences. Fola LaFollette is an example of one such teacher who student taught at City and Country before her four-year career as a teacher there and who was an articulate proponent of Miss Pratt and her philosophy. Jean Wessen Murray began her 44 years of service in 1934 with student teaching under Miss Pratt's guidance and went on to become a principal in 1948. She faithfully carried out the school's philosophy for the next 30 years. Leila Stott was also a loyal supporter of Miss Pratt and her vision. She taught at City and Country for many years. These teachers (and others) constituted what some teachers felt was an "in group of discipleship" which was difficult to enter.

Elsie Ripley Clapp, reflecting on the 1923-24 school year that she spent as a teacher of the XIIs, definitely felt that she was not "one of them."[55] The impression that was given, according to Elsie, was that one couldn't understand the school's philosophy in only a year, especially without the experience of teaching younger groups. It raises a question of the difficulty novice teachers must have had until Miss Pratt and the staff of the "in group" accepted them.

Clapp's unease at City and Country was undoubtedly compounded by Miss Pratt's negative stance toward academe. Elsie believed that Pratt maintained a bias against her because of her college education and professional relationship with John Dewey. One of the conditions of Clapp's employment was that she spend two mornings a week working with Dewey at Teachers College. "During the winter and spring sessions she assisted Dewey in two courses, Logic and Educational Problems and Historic Relations of Philosophy and Education."[56] The fact that Clapp worked closely with a leader in progressive education who Miss Pratt felt never paid attention to her school probably played a part in the resentment Clapp felt.[57] Miss Pratt's somewhat off-putting interactions with Clapp are consistent with her belief that the best teachers were those who did not have formal training in pedagogy and curriculum. Teachers such as Clapp were more focused on lesson content and delivery than on facilitating the child's learning process, that latter being more valued by Pratt.

She also felt that Miss Pratt didn't like her because she was able to handle her own discipline of a group of children that had been considered difficult by previous teachers. Admittedly, it was a rambunctious group that "sent me to bed immediately after supper during the first three months...." Clapp reported that after responding to what they were interested in studying, "by midyear life began to be much pleasanter for everyone."[58]

Miss Pratt's manner was not always authoritarian, however. A teacher who worked under her commented, "One of her strong points was that she didn't hinder the ideas of others as long as it didn't interfere with the children's education. What teachers did with their political lives outside of the school was okay." An example of this is a situation in which Miss Pratt initially saw a teacher's politics as interfering. She wrote about it in her personal journal (1933-34 school year). She was very direct in opposing the teacher who wanted a change of assignment the following year,..."whereupon I fell upon her and said I would never trust her with the XIIs because of her radical interpretation of history...and toward present day economics." Nevertheless, several journal entries later, she acknowledged her acquiescence to the change the teacher wanted.

Despite Miss Pratt's self-described autocratic management style, a democratic structure of school governance was put in place as the school grew larger. It was incorporated in 1924 as a teacher's cooperative and received the last such charter in the state of New York. All the teachers who had completed one year of service were members of the cooperative, which was governed by a five member executive committee. The principal, secretary, and treasurer of the school were the officers of the corporation and they annually elected the other two staff members who would serve on the executive committee. Miss Pratt was always elected president.

In addition to the business meetings, regular teachers' meetings were also held. One function of this group was to decide on the educational value of materials that were being considered for inclusion in the classrooms. "What could it do for the self-image, confidence, and creativity of the children? Was it manageable? How much learning was inherent in the material?" These were some questions that one of the teachers recalled addressing during these sessions.[59] An example from a 1922 record is illustrative: The staff was considering purchasing maps with celluloid overlays that outlined additional features of the geographic information. Miss Pratt "wondered if the overlays were predigesting material for the children and if they [the children] ought to make them themselves."[60] Mrs. Mitchell and other staff members were able to convince her that the overlays only covered the most basic information, and that the purchase would not compromise the children's learning.

Miss Pratt's leadership skills did not include being a good fiscal manager. She had little money herself, and no sense of it for running the school. A comment she made in one letter in a series of exchanges with Lucy Sprague Mitchell regarding taxes on the City and Country School property confirmed this. "I am stupid about figures and probably try to shift consideration of them to others,"[61] was Miss Pratt's excuse for her inattention to the problem. It was said that she believed so strongly in her school that she just knew it would be supported financially. She looked to others who shared her vision to provide the money to advance her work. Lucy Sprague Mitchell, who provided financial support during the early years of the school, echoed that view: "Pratt had such intense belief in her experiment that she felt the world owed it support."[62] Evelyn Baldwin, the wife of ACLU founder Roger Baldwin and a City and Country parent, was another benefactor of the school in its lean years during the Depression, "when City and Country teachers were teaching and learning from children out of their own pockets."[63] In other words, several teachers gave all or part of their salaries back to the school. Baldwin provided a second mortgage to the school at a very low rate.[64] The City and Country budget for 1929-30 is illustrative of the lean years of the Depression. A $2,354 deficit was noted even though a grant from the Keith Fund paid for books and the librarian's salary of $2,300. Lucy Sprague Mitchell made what was probably her last donation of $11,600 that year and did not take a salary according to the budget. Miss Pratt's salary was $5,000.[65] During this school year, Mitchell also sold the three buildings the school occupied to the school adding to the personal financial loss she had incurred because of the Depression.[66] Although the terms of the sale were generous, it still represented a serious financial burden for the school in this economically difficult period.

The City and Country School's financial picture remained bleak for several years. In a letter to Fola LaFollette, January 4, 1932, Pratt wrote about the future of the school looking lean financially. She quite cavalierly described a finance committee, "organized at their own suggestion and I am going to give up that end of it!" One can only wonder how the finance committee members were able to convince Miss Pratt to withdraw from this area of school administration. But, she just might have had enough fund raising! One of her diary entries talks about how many thank you letters she had written to benefactors for contributions which had ranged so far from 2 to 100 dollars.[67]

The finance committee may have been responsible for a 1936 fundraiser that boasted a star-studded cast. Records indicated that George Gershwin contributed the music and was in the cast, George S. Kaufman wrote a script, Dorothy Parker contributed a scene, and Gypsy Rose Lee made a guest appearance. This was probably not the only way the school capitalized on the resources of its artistic and creative community.

Nowadays, the idea of a feminist style of leadership is discussed in the literature and applied to women leaders who demonstrate behaviors of care, concern, and connection. However, in the early part of the century, feminist thought and practice didn't seem to deal with leadership. It was more concerned with the development of the individual woman. According to Kate Wittenstein, who researched the Heterodoxy organization, the idea of freedom for women was a strong focus of early twentieth-century feminism. An obstacle to women's freedom was custom and tradition and convention, and Caroline Pratt's professional life demonstrated an obvious disregard for these obstacles.

The school was run as a cooperative, which might lead some to believe that consensus was used for decision making. While that may have applied in some situations such as deciding on materials and equipment for the classrooms, it was not used across the board. The fact that Caroline Pratt was elected the president of the executive committee each year indicates that she was the ultimate decision maker.

She did fit the pattern of school leaders in the progressive tradition. The women school leaders were strong, visionary, and often charismatic. Their motivation for establishing a school was generally to right social and educational wrongs through an academic and socially based curriculum. They were instrumental in fundraising for the school, and generally drew a group of loyal parents and teachers around them.

Notes

1. ILFC, 40.
2. Mumford, *Sketches from Life: The Autobiography of Lewis Mumford.*
3. Cremin, *The Transformation of the School,* 206.
4. Beck, "Progressive Education and American Progressivism: Caroline Pratt," 129-137.
5. CP and Lucille Demming, "Experimental Schools, The Play School," in Charlotte Winsor, ed., *Experimental Schools Revisited: Bulletins of the Bureau of Educational Experiments.*
6. ILFC, 58.
7. Cremin, *The Transformation of the School,* 206.
8. CCSA, unpublished manuscript, binder of CP publications. n.d.
9. CP, "Making Environment Meaningful," 105.
10. The zone of proximal development is defined as the distance between the actual developmental level as determined by independent problem solving and the level of potential development as determined through problem solving under

adult guidance or in collaboration with more capable peers. Vygotsky, *Mind and Society*, 86.

11. CP, "Two Basic Principles of Education," 175.
12. ILFC, 8.
13. See section: "The Play School Begins"
14. The classes at the City and Country School are grouped according to the age of the children, denoted by Roman numerals. Groups III and IV are preschool children, Group V is the kindergarten age group, Group VI is the first grade level, etc.
15. CP, "Jobs and How They Have Been Chosen," 1.
16. ILFC, 101.
17. Delahanty and May, "The Place of Reading and Social Science in a Job-Centered School," 7.
18. CP, "Jobs and How They Have Been Chosen," 1.
19. Stott, "Teachers in War Time," *Progressive Education*.
20. Semel, "Lessons from the Past," 69.
21. ILFC, 130.
22. CP, "As to Indoctrination, 108.
23. CP, Forward to: "The Place of Reading and Social Science in a Job-Centered School."
24. Ibid., 1.
25. ILFC, 193.
26. Ibid., 80.
27. Ibid.
28. LC, Fola LaFollette Collection, Box E153.
29. ILFC, 194.
30. CP, "Two Basic Principles of Education," 175.
31. CCSA RG9.5, Box 1, folder 14.
32. Elsie Ripley Clapp Memoirs, 206, used with permission.
33. CP, "Two Basic Principles of Education," 175.
34. ILFC, 8.
35. MML, Bank Street Collection. Mary Marot was a social worker who had been one of the first New York School Visitors.
36. CU, Lucy Sprague Mitchell Collection, oral history interview, 1962.
37. The labels and descriptions of the curriculum plan vary slightly in different references.
38. LC, Fola LaFollette Section.
39. ILFC, 192.
40. Ibid., 196.
41. CCSA, Caroline Pratt diary. May 3, 1935.
42. CCSA.
43. CCSA, Letter to Mrs. M.B., June 1, 1938.
44. CCSA, Letter from Mrs. M.B., September, 6, 1948.
45. CCSA, untitled typed draft, RG3.2.4 Box 6, folder 12.
46. ILFC 185.
47. Ibid., 183.
48. Ibid., 182.
49. CP, *Experimental Practice in the City and Country School*, 2.

50. CCSA.

51. ILFC, 178.

52. Stack, *Elsie Ripley Clapp*, 130.

53. Carlton, "Caroline Pratt: A Biography," 234.

54. Semel, "Female Founders and the Progressive Paradox," 92-96.

55. Elsie Ripley Clapp Memoirs, 208.

56. Stack, *Elsie Ripley Clapp*, 129.

57. Ibid., 130.

58. Ibid., 129.

59. Caplan and Caplan, *The Power of Play*, 271.

60. CCSA Binder of Library History.

61. CCSA, letter dated April 16, 1934.

62. Mitchell, *Two Lives*, 412.

63. CCSA, Evelyn Preston's eulogy by Mary B. Piel. June 19, 1962. It appeared that the practice of teachers "teaching and learning from children out of their own pockets" occurred at other times besides the Depression years. For the month of February 1926, school records indicated that Miss Pratt received only half of her salary returning half to cover a deficit. Her annual salary for the 1925-26 school year was $5,000 and remained at that amount at least through 1930.

64. Ibid.

65. LC., Fola LaFollette Section. Both letters quoted are in this archive.

66. Details of this sale and the acrimony surrounding it are discussed in Antler, *Lucy Sprague Mitchell, The Making of a Modern Woman*, based on information in Mitchell's unpublished autobiography and biography, *Two Lives*.

67. CCSA, Caroline Pratt diary, April 17, 1935.

Figure 14. Caroline Pratt at her desk

CHAPTER EIGHT

Caroline Pratt's Influence in the Progressive Education Community

I have believed too deeply in the right of children to grow
and learn...not to wish that other teachers besides our staff...would dedicate
themselves to...rescuing children from the dead hand
of traditional education.[1]

CAROLINE PRATT'S INDEPENDENT THINKING was reflected in her professional associations as well as in her work at the City and Country School. She was definitely a visible member of the progressive education community in New York City, but she was cautious about the alliances that she made and maintained lest she be put into an ideological box that did not suit her. For example, she maintained only a marginal connection with the Progressive Education Association (PEA), founded in 1919. However, she did contribute several articles to its journal, *Progressive Education*. (See listings in Appendix B.)

It is possible that the organizations with which she affiliated were ones in which she could maintain some control of her ideals in relation to the work of the group. She was a part of two other smaller, more focused organizations that promoted the philosophies of progressive education: The New York Society for the Experimental Study of Education and the Associated Experimental Schools. The former was organized about 1926, and its membership included some of the women who were considered the most "outspoken advocates of progressivism in the New York area."[2]

The Associated Experimental Schools, of which she was a founder, began in the fall of 1934. Member schools were City and Country, Hessian Hills, Little Red Schoolhouse, Manumit, Coop School for Student Teachers (predecessor of Bank Street College),

Harriet Johnson Nursery School, (formerly called BEE Nursery School) and the Walden School, all New York area schools.[3] The purpose of this group was to seek to establish a cooperative rather than a competitive environment in schools: no marks, rewards, or honors. Rather they advocated evaluating children individually in comparison with past performance. Educational success was determined by the richness of the children's experiences rather than by the amount of factual information acquired. The organization was based on the premise that learning is a growth process. It is more than the acquisition of knowledge. Schools should be concerned with the whole child, and should adapt to his or her needs at each stage of development. This premise led to providing the time and materials for the child to discover, develop, and express his/her own meanings and relationships. Real jobs were advocated to extend children's social horizons and increase their capacity for cooperative action. Clearly this organization's philosophy was very compatible with Caroline Pratt's own ideas.[4]

Presentations and Publications

Championing progressive education and promoting the City and Country School philosophy and practice were Miss Pratt's passions. Despite her unwillingness to formalize and codify an educational theory for dissemination in books and journals, there is ample documentation that her ideas were frequently in the public eye. Her first major publication, *Experimental Practice in the City and Country School*, came out in 1924 and was reviewed in *Progressive Education* by Agnes De Lima, a well known progressive educator. De Lima reported that "it represents a first statement of aims and practices by a pioneer in experimental schooling who for ten years has been saying little but achieving much in a relatively unexplored field."[5] While this was generally a descriptive review, the following year, De Lima published a book about progressive education in which she raised some questions about educational practices at the City and Country School.[6]

Fola LaFollette's personal papers contain a record of a conference convened by Miss Pratt at the City and Country School in March 1928 on the topic of "The Use of the Environment in the Elementary School Curriculum."[7] The conference was attended by both private and public school teachers. Lucy Sprague Mitchell reported on how geography was taught at City and Country through the use of direct, hands-on experiences. She lamented the fact that all she had to show were the products of the work, but that the most important part was the habits of thinking and acting which were developed by the children through their construction and use of the projects. She explained that geography was taught by studying the relationship of facts rather than the classification of them. The notes of the conversation that occurred after the presentations indicated areas of common concern among the participants, despite the differing practices in each school. The discussions centered on how to postpone the teaching of reading and how to adapt public school programs to be more progressive.[8]

In 1930 and 1931 the PEA sponsored a series of radio talks to publicize their work. Caroline Pratt shared the microphone with other progressive education luminaries such as James Heard Kilpatrick and George Counts of Teachers College; Robert Leigh, president of Bennington College; Florence Cane, art teacher at the Walden School; and Howard Nudd, the director of the Public Education Association of New York City.[9]

Miss Pratt was also a contributor to a series of articles in the *New Republic* that ran for six consecutive issues in 1930 under the heading of "The New Education: Ten Years After." The series was described as "a general discussion of progressive education in the United States—its achievements thus far, its present dangers and promises for the future." John Dewey was also a contributor, as was Margaret Naumberg, founder of the progressive Walden School, Joseph K. Hart, a University of Wisconsin professor of education, and Boyd Bode, an Ohio State University professor. Miss Pratt's article, "Two Basic Principles of Education," defined two principles of the new education, the idea that programs "be experiencing ones" and the premise that these programs spring from children's experiences in work and play. She provided examples of how these principles were enacted at the City and Country School through block building activities for the younger children and dramatics and the jobs program for the older groups.

Her personal column in the first issue of a school publication, *The City and Country School Bulletin Board* in April 1936 contained two accounts of her outreach efforts. She wrote of "an example of opportunities which our school likes to have and takes advantage of" describing Manumit School staff coming to City and Country school on a Saturday morning to discuss their curriculum. This led to a second meeting after which a proposed reorganization of their program was submitted for her review. The second account concerned the development of an afternoon play and work curriculum in the public schools which is described in a following section, "Public School Connections."

Another column, *Across the Principal's Desk,* described the national and international correspondence that was regularly received asking for help with educational problems. "Today one [letter] may arrive from the State Central Institute for Scientific Research in Moscow asking for specifications and suggestions on play equipment for young children; tomorrow a request from the Czecho-Slovak Ministry of Schools and National Education for an exhibit of children's art and printed materials."[10] The column also reported that filling such requests was difficult because of the lack of staff and necessary funds to do so. Nevertheless, the school "feels that it can only fulfill its primary function as an educational experiment when it is able to build up the additional support needed to make it possible to offer its findings to anyone and everyone who can use them." This attitude exemplifies Miss Pratt's passion for sharing her school's program as well as her lack of business sense. A more entrepreneurial principal might have marketed the "products" of the school with an eye to financial as well as ideological gain.

Her personal diary of 1934-1935 provides other examples of her outreach activities. On November 23 she gave a speech at the regional Progressive Education Conference at the Waldorf Astoria Hotel. Just ten days later, she entered the following: "Went to Little Red [The Little Red Schoolhouse, a progressive school in New York City], met her [principal Elisabeth Irwin] staff, had tea and read part of my paper on Educational Frontiers.[11] Very interesting discussion."

School Visitors

In addition to sending letters requesting information about the City and Country School, educators and others interested in how Caroline Pratt implemented progressive education learned about her school and came to visit. The 1927 annual report of the school recorded 505 visitors—307 educators (teachers and administrators), 53 parents and 145 miscellaneous. It is interesting to speculate on the nature of the group labeled miscellaneous—possibly college students, health workers, or psychologists.

A four-year record of visitors for the 1931-1935 school years was kept according to home location. It indicated a significant increase in visitations: 1,555 people visited from 45 different states and 1,600 visitors came from foreign countries in Europe, the Middle East and Asia.[12] Since that would make an overall average of nearly 631 visitors a year, one could raise a question about the accuracy of the numbers. Based on an eight-month school year and a 20-day school month, the school would be receiving about 20 visitors each and every week, a large number of people to accommodate while maintaining the daily school routine.

Her diary, which covers her activities during part of this period, does have frequent references to visitors, so the numbers above may not be exaggerated. For example: "The Union Theological Seminary came (They come every year). Eight visitors in this group" (November 19, 1934). In April 1935, she recorded visitors from Montreal, Canada; Scarsdale, New York; Sweden, and New York University. She also recorded the following exchange with visitors:

> Two puzzled public school teachers from Sunnyside were steered into my office to question me particularly about reading. They had seen no formal work at all and wondered if we did any. They had been with the 7s, following them to library, cooking, and shop. I tried to find formal work going on somewhere in the school but it was too late. It was well over except for a class in the 11s in which Margaret Ernst was having word analysis. This was reassuring to them and they left saying they had a few things to try out and would come back for more! (exclamation in original).

The formal work that the teachers wanted to see was the direct instruction that was typically delivered in most traditional classrooms. It is not surprising that Miss Pratt had trouble providing an example of this practice in any classroom in her school.

Public School Connections

Having her ideas about teaching and learning accepted into public schools was a goal that Miss Pratt maintained throughout her career. She could easily have been satisfied with the success of the City and Country School in effectively preparing students for high school and college work. But the students she originally set out to teach, the children of immigrant families, remained in her thinking. Working with public schools would enable her to once again serve these students.

The first connection made with public schools was in 1935 with the Putnam Valley Central School, a newly consolidated township school, in Putnam County near Lake Peekskill. One play program and one service job was attempted that year in this school. Miss Pratt and Leila Stott, a member of the City and Country school faculty, acted as the school's consultants, and Miss Stott spent a considerable amount of time at the school setting up the program. She established a play program for the first and second grades and a jobs program for third and fourth graders that involved making rag rugs for the younger students' rest period. The administration and teachers were very supportive and willing to accept the ideas of progressive educational practice and felt that the program "made the educational system richer and our children happier."[13]

Miss Stott became the chief ambassador of the City and Country School's philosophy and innovative educational practices. In addition to the work at the Putnam Valley School, she reported consultations with schools in Pennsylvania and New York.[14] These consultations involved just a visit or two. The report also cites the fact that the work with public schools has been received by the State Education Department in Albany with a "cordial attitude." "The Rural Division has been especially interested in seeing a new type of curriculum worked out for a rural school and have asked for a report of our results for publication."[15] Miss Stott's work in organizing school programs was even mentioned in her obituary.[16]

Another public school connection was made in New York City. Mrs. Moses Blitzer, a City and Country School parent, was instrumental in establishing this connection. At the end of the school day in urban neighborhoods she had observed "swarms of children playing in the street...[and] the neighborhood school building...its rooms empty, its doors closed."[17] She felt that participating in a program such as carried out at the City and Country School would be a more productive use of children's time between 3 and 5 p.m. than being idle and hanging around on the street. Many mothers of immigrant families were at work, and their children were at loose ends until parents returned home from work.

Beginning in 1936, New York PS 33 in Chelsea at 418 W. 28th St., partnered with City and Country School to develop an after school program. This school was selected because the educational philosophy of the principal, Miss Ruth Gillette Hardy, was compatible with that of the City and Country School. Another criterion for selection was a building that was older and adaptable to the program. The organizing committee "wanted to prove that children's happiness is quite independent of 'fancy quarters'—that 'any school can do it.'"[18]

The program began on a shoestring, with donated materials and volunteer help. The City and Country School provided used blocks for the all-important block building activities. Volunteers, recruited from the ranks of City and Country School parents, members of the Parents Organization of PS 33, members of the Junior League, and other friends of the program received in-service training at the City and Country School. Students from several teacher training programs in New York also participated by doing fieldwork at PS 33.

The children were grouped according to ages and joined "clubs" that featured such activities as carpentry, travel (field trips around the city), dance, industrial arts, and city explorers (a version of the travel club for older children). All the clubs included outdoor play, music and rhythms, and refreshments.

The goal was to serve 300 of the school's 1,200 students, and after the first year Miss Hardy was so impressed with the results on the children that she wanted as many as possible to be included in the following year. She saw the children show "a gain in poise, in responsibility; they were more relaxed, more responsive."[19] She also wanted to have a fulltime person from the City and Country School to help all of the teachers who desired to incorporate some of the methods into their classrooms.

Other connections were to follow. In a note to Fola LaFollete in January 1942, Caroline wrote, "Our greatest excitement [at City and Country School] is over our entrance to the public schools. With the backing of the Board of Education, we are starting work in two big public schools in Harlem next month."[20] One of these was PS 194 whose principal, Mr. Daniel G. Krane, also supported modern educational and recreational methods.

These schools were known as the All Day Neighborhood Schools and were to be demonstration sites for other New York schools. Funded by the Public Education Association and other community agencies, the focus was to provide a program of after school activities for children in high crime areas. Rather than remedial teaching after school, the program provided activities children could both master and enjoy. The confidence this program established heightened the children's incentive to pursue their studies as they learned to understand that many gratifications depend on the ability to master specific skills and disciplines. In areas where the school functioned, the crime rate markedly dropped.[21]

Caroline was very proud of these public school programs. Their success verified for her that the City and Country philosophy and curriculum was "good for children everywhere and of every kind, children who have apple trees to climb as well as children who carry the door key of a tenement flat on a string around their necks."[22] Apparently "latch key children" could not be blamed on the women's liberation movement of the 1960s and 1970s. Even in the 1930s children went to empty houses after school.

Caroline was one of 18 citizens recognized in *The Nation* magazine's 1939 Roll of Honor for extending her school philosophy and practices to the public schools.[23] The citation read as follows:

> *Caroline Pratt, founder of the City and Country School*
> *Whose devotion to the principles of progressive education won their acceptance*
> *in the organization of a number of public schools in New York State.*

This award was especially satisfying to her because it acknowledged her work with public schools. Successfully applying her ideas to public schools represented the pinnacle of educational success, and she knew that success would bring wider acceptance of her progressive agenda.

Alternative Views of Caroline Pratt's Ideas

Probably the one commonality shared by schools that considered themselves progressive, or exponents of the New Education, was their opposition to what they referred to as traditional education. It was often cited as a major shortcoming of the movement—the fact that while it was easy to understand what progressive schools were *against*, it was not easy to describe a common set of ideas that they stood *for*. This situation also made it difficult to evaluate a progressive school because there was no commonly held definition of progressive education. This can be considered both a strength and a weakness. On one hand, it enables schools to devise a variety of formats to meet the needs of their students, but on the other, it begs the question of how to determine what a "good" progressive school looks like. For example, child-centeredness seems to be a consistent descriptor of progressive schools, yet how the school enacts a curriculum (or lack of curriculum) to be child-centered is very much an individual choice.

The lack of agreement among progressive schools was recalled by Charlotte Winsor, a former teacher at City and Country School, in reviewing the early days of New York progressive schools. "Schools had already established themselves with a wide range of philosophical backgrounds and ideas. It's hard to believe that in 1924 they were already fighting with each other about conceptual things and what we mean by progressive education. And the City and Country School, which I think was a profound reflection of these new ideas, was at that time being attacked by some other progressive school crowd as being over-intellectualized....This was not true freedom for the child. City and Country was not really progressive because they had a curriculum. That we had a curriculum and, that of all the dreadful things, teachers were expected to write out their curriculum goals at the beginning of the year. This distressed the critics."[24]

In her 1926 book, *Our Enemy the Child*, Agnes De Lima drew on examples from the City and Country School, among others, to illustrate programs that demonstrated the progressive principles she advocated. But she did, very diplomatically, put forth some criticisms of Miss Pratt's ideas. "There are, of course, certain matters in Miss Pratt's school about which perhaps more discussion is needed."[25] She identified four matters which she discussed with great deference and respect. The first was related to Charlotte Winsor's comments above regarding the tension between a child-centered school philosophy and the existence of a curriculum plan. Ms. De Lima wrote, "It is possible that under less wise leadership, Miss Pratt's insistence upon program making might result in too great formalism." She also alluded to the nature of the curriculum with the observation, "Miss Pratt has also been occasionally criticized for limiting the development of imagination by keeping the children too much in the present and giving them too much concrete material."

The organization of the school was called into question with this comment, "One might also question whether the very complete classification of children by chronological age, and the formulating of activities according to varying age levels is not injecting something at once spurious and artificial." Finally, "Advances in analytic psychology may also modify Miss Pratt's very emphatic contention that there is something 'unfortunate' about a child who does not 'attack' materials, but instead has his interest 'riveted' in people."[26]

Critical observations of progressive education in general, in addition to the perceived lack of curriculum mentioned above, were reported by Harold Rugg and Ann Schumacher. They included schools following too slavishly the interests of individual children, overemphasis on one or another of the subjects, and a lack of assessment of their programs.[27] While applying these criticisms is a subjective process, it appeared that only one of them could be leveled against the City and Country School. There was a strong presence of the social studies in the curriculum which could be considered an overemphasis. The field trips and other investigations related to the activities of the jobs program provided a strong focus on areas contained in the social studies, particularly history, geography, and economics.

The emphasis on creative self-expression that guided the programs in some progressive schools led, in the view of some critics, from liberty to license, from spontaneity to planlessness, from individuality to recalcitrance, and from education to chaos.[28] A *New Yorker* magazine cartoon captured the critical view some took of teaching in progressive classrooms. The cartoon pictures a schoolboy who asks, "Do we have to do what we want to do today?"[29]

Miss Pratt was not immune to these criticisms, but she did not see her school as meriting the kind of criticism handed out by some traditionalists. For example, she would not have accepted the perspective that progressive schools were intent on "guarding the child against strain in the learning process."[30] Nor would she interpret the idea of freedom for children as license to behave as they chose. Rather than addressing her critics with rhetoric, she chose to demonstrate the learning of the students at City and Country through carefully kept individual and group records as well as keeping track of the performance of City and Country's graduates. The question of how City and Country graduates fare when they enter high school is consistently answered as "very well." Leo Huberman, basing his information on the first 115 graduates of the school, reported, "That they do well is sufficiently proven by the fact that they continue to be welcomed by every school which has ever enrolled any of the graduates....City and Country graduates are student leaders in the thick of every school battle [academic as well as athletic and social]."[31] Huberman invited doubters to come and look at the grades and letters of recommendation provided by headmasters and principals that the school keeps on file. Such information enabled Miss Pratt to boast that her school did indeed serve as a child's laboratory that satisfied a vital inborn love of research and investigation.

She wrote, "The slogan of such a school is, 'we learn from experience.' From our own observations, carried on for twenty years, of children carving out their own education, we believe there is no better method."[32]

Notes

1. ILFC, 176.
2. Graham, *Progressive Education: From Arcady to Academe*, 44.
3. "News from the Field" *Progressive Education*, January 1936.
4. Caroline Pratt was also a founder of the Bureau of Educational Experiments (BEE) that was described in Chapter Five. Since this organization was developed around the City and Country School's philosophy, it was also an organization in which she could maintain some control over its work. She was active in the BEE until differences in philosophy between Lucy Sprague Mitchell and herself necessitated a parting of the ways.
5. *Progressive Education* 2, (1925), 51.
6. See section: "Alternative Views of Caroline Pratt's Ideas" in this chapter.
7. LC, Fola LaFollette Section.
8. This conference also could have occurred in 1927. There is inconsistency in various references to it.

9. Graham, *From Arcady to Academe*, 88.

10. CCSA, *The City and Country School Bulletin Board*, 1:1 (1936), 3.

11. Unfortunately, a paper with this title was not located in the CCSA.

12. Hirsch, "Caroline Pratt and the City and Country School, 1914-1945," 95.

13. CCSA, Jean Murray box.

14. CCSA, *City and Country School Bulletin Board* (1,4) lists these schools: the Miquon School near Philadelphia and the School in Rose Valley at Moylan, PA; The Sunnyside School in Long Island City, The Stevens Junior School in Germantown, and the Harley School in Rochester, NY.

15. Ibid., 4.

16. CCSA, Jean Murray box.

17. Franklin and Benedict, *Play Centers for School Children*, 1. This book contains a detailed description of the PS 33 center.

18. Ibid., 2.

19. Ibid., 4.

20. LC. Fola LaFollete Section, Box E10.

21. CCSA, Jean Murray Box.

22. ILFC, 177.

23. CCSA.

24. CU. Lucy Sprague Mitchell Collection, Box 4. These comments were taken from the transcription of a taped conversation with Charlotte Winsor and others.

25. De Lima, *Our Enemy the Child*, 156.

26. Ibid., 156, 157.

27. Cremin, *Transformation of the School*, 279.

28. Ibid., 207.

29. Bode, *Progressive Education at the Crossroads*, 99.

30. Graham, *From Arcady to Academe*, 102.

31. *The City and Country School Bulletin Board*, 1 (April, 1936).

32. CP, "Learning by Experience," *Child Study*, 71.

CHAPTER NINE

The Private Caroline Pratt

I'm not up to talking much.[1]

CAROLINE PRATT'S TERSE PROTESTATION, included in an interview published in the *Vineyard Gazette* on July 30, 1937, encapsulates her reticence about sharing personal information. It helps to shed some light on the difficulty of answering the question, What was the private Miss Pratt like? How did she spend her time when she wasn't working at the City and Country School? Little has been recorded about her life outside of her role as the school founder and principal, which gives the impression that her professional interests were one in the same with her personal interactions. The dearth of information also makes contradictions in reports difficult to verify. For example, during the period that Lucy Sprague Mitchell and Caroline Pratt worked together at the City and Country School, Mitchell's biographer Joyce Antler recorded that the women visited together constantly. They went to the theatre together, often spent weekends together at the Hopewell Junction Farm or at the Mitchell's vacation cottages, and shared holiday meals. However, a former student who was in the same class as Mitchell's son Sprague, recalled that while his family was often invited to the Mitchells' house for Thanksgiving, Miss Pratt and Helen Marot were not present.

Creating the proper context for the sparse information that is available is another difficulty in representing Miss Pratt's out-of-school life. Some examples follow: In 1928 she traveled to Europe to attend the International Conference on the New Education in France, accompanied by Helen Marot, and friends Rachel Scott and her husband, artist Bill Scott. Did Miss Pratt present a paper at this conference? Was she part of an American delegation?

Dinners with Lewis and Sophia Mumford were recorded in Mumford's autobiography, but are not evident in writings of either Pratt or Marot. Were these restaurant meals? Were they at the Mumford home? Were they part of a larger group of people? Because so many questions remain unanswered, the the following sections represent an admittedly incomplete story of Caroline Pratt's private life.

Personal Friendships

Members of the City and Country School staff who knew her reported that Miss Pratt was a private person and "didn't socialize much." Few staff members were "close" to her. Most of her personal friends, according to evidence pieced together from a variety of sources, were members of the arts and literary community. However, her friendships with some of these members of the creative community were also bound up with the school. Either the children became enrolled because of the parents' friendship with Miss Pratt or the adult friendships developed when the children attended City and Country. For example, information from Thomas Hart Benton's autobiography indicated that his children were enrolled in the school in exchange for his teaching art. Friends Roger Baldwin, founder of the American Civil Liberties Union, and Evelyn Preston Baldwin were neighbors who also sent their children to the City and Country School. The Baldwins had a home on Martha's Vineyard and Miss Pratt and Helen Marot socialized with them there in the summers.

In addition to these friendships that included a connection to her school, Carlton's biography lists a group of people with whom Caroline was personally acquainted; however, the extent of these acquaintances was not discussed. All of them were writers, artists, or people involved in the New York theatre scene.[2] Some of this group were also zealous socialists; others, as mentioned earlier, were members of the feminist group Heterodoxy. Anne Herendeen, a writer and editor, was a Heterodoxy member who Caroline mentioned in her 1933-34 journal. In addition to spending social time together, Caroline wrote that Anne also supplied editorial advice on an article she was preparing for publication.

A brief reference to her relationship with Margaret Sanger was found in a biography of Sanger.[3] Caroline and Helen cared for two of Sanger's children, Grant, age six, and Peggy, four and a half, for a brief time when Sanger fled the country in 1914 in order to avoid prosecution for her activities in support of birth control for women.

How long they stayed with Caroline and Helen is not clear, but the account indicates that the children missed their parents so much that their father Bill had to retrieve them and get a relative to live with them to be a caregiver while Margaret was in Europe. A third son Stuart, age eleven, was away at boarding school at the time.

Correspondence that documented a friendship bridging the professional/personal divide was found in letters between Caroline and Fola LaFollete, a teacher at the City and Country School. Fola taught between 1926 and 1930; and after she left the school, their correspondence and some infrequent visits continued until Caroline's death. The correspondence showed mutual warmth for one another. Interestingly, the content of most of Caroline's letters to Fola dealt primarily with school-related happenings even after Caroline retired as principal, another indication of the central role of the City and Country School in her identity.

Found in the papers of Fola's husband, playwright George Middleton, was a brief undated handwritten note from Caroline:

> Dear George Middleton,
> I want to tell you that your play still remains with me. I liked it unreservedly. So much that it seemed to be entirely beside the point to make any criticism because it could only be a trivial one. I had a delightful evening and wanted again to thank you and Fola.
> Sincerely, Caroline Pratt.[4]

From this note we can learn that Caroline attended the theatre, maybe frequently, since she had a number of friends who were connected with theatre production. It is also another example of Caroline's direct style of communication.

Caroline's friend and fellow educator, Jean Wesson Murray, explained in a 1976 interview Hirsch conducted for her dissertation that while Caroline was sympathetic to social and feminist causes and gained strength from the encouragement (and in some cases, financial support) of feminist friends, she kept these political views separate from her work with children.[5] Murray also told Hirsch that educators such as Elisabeth Irwin, Harriet Johnson, and Margaret Naumberg interacted with one another and respected one another's work. Though their ideas and methodologies differed, these women derived common support from one another in their various ways of differing from their common enemy—traditional education.[6]

According to Lucy Sprague Mitchell's biographer, Joyce Antler, Caroline labeled herself a revolutionary socialist. Antler described this position as a "radical vision of a new social order to which the child, taught to think properly, held the key."[7] Antler quotes from an early position paper on socialist education that Caroline had written, emphasizing pedagogy as defining socialist education:

> A socialist education would first of all recognize that the method of gaining knowledge through the medium of books exclusively is obsolete. Also, confining a child to expressing himself through written language exclusively is obsolete. The Socialist would throw down these methods as completely as he throws down the method of competition in industry. What is needed is revolution and the keynote is the application of a new method as fundamental as the one employed to bring about the cooperative commonwealth.[8]

It can be assumed that her years of association with Helen Marot, beginning in Philadelphia in the late 1890s, her socialist friends, and her membership in the Women's Trade Union League, were responsible for this ideology. Caroline joined this organization in the early 1900s shortly after moving to New York, and served as treasurer for several years.

Max Eastman described Helen and Caroline as "two charming sophisticated old maids" in his autobiography. At the time of this reference the women were in their mid-forties. They occupied a "diminutive red house on Thirteenth Street just west of Seventh avenue."[9] Eastman, his wife Ida Rauh, who was a good friend of Helen, and their son Daniel lived in a small house at the back of the lot. Ida Rauh was an active member of the Women's Trade Union League, which Helen had helped to found in 1903. This house was one of several that the two women shared, all very close to the City and Country School.

Summer Retreats

Caroline and Helen purchased a farm of about 100 acres in Beckett, Massachusetts, an isolated area in the Berkshires, on June 12, 1905. The deed stated, "Said grantor reserves the right to enter and care for and harvest his crop of oats and potatoes already planted on granted premises."[10] Apparently those were the last crops grown on the farm, because there is no record that the women continued the farming operation. In fact, there is no record of any of their activities on the farm. A terse paragraph in a *New York Times* column, "In a Few Words," provides no additional information. It simply reported that "Helen Marot has a 100 acre farm near Becket Centre, Mass, where she spends her summers, returning to New York for autumn and winter."[11] The farm was sold on January 7, 1926. Their following summers were to be spent on the Atlantic shore.

In 1924 Caroline purchased land on Martha's Vineyard Island and the following year she built a cottage on Memensha Pond. She and Helen were among the first summer residents of this part of the island, a very different environment than the more upscale eastern end.

Memensha Pond was part of a colorful fishing port area on the western end of the island in Chilmark, an isolated fishing and farming community. The area was noted for its deserted windswept beaches, and undulating gray stone walls rolling over the moors and reaching down to the sea. The artist Thomas Hart Benton, a friend of Caroline and Helen, first came to Martha's Vineyard in 1920 and later, he too, purchased a summer home. In his biography, the area is described as one of extraordinary beauty which "more than compensated for the crude living conditions which contrasted so sharply with the summer colonies on the eastern end of the island."[12] In the summer of 1920, it was reported that there were only three indoor toilets, very little electricity and a 25 party line phone system.

Benton's wife Rita recalled that because in those days the summer residents in Chilmark were so few they did many things together. Many of the get-togethers were in the Bentons' home. "These were always highly talkative and were mostly directed, as the major interests of the time dictated, to the social and political problems of America or, because of a number of teachers in our set, to the question of American education, which was then much affected by the struggles between John Deweyites, Marxist radicals, and extreme conservatives."[13]

Friends Lewis and Sophia Mumford also summered in the area. It seemed that the area didn't change much in the seven years between Benton's account and this one written by Mumford in 1927. He described the "primitive living:" a shabby little shack, an outhouse 60-70 feet away from the cottage, and the spring from which water had to be drawn, even farther [away]. Neighbors "were scattered about the landscape," Helen Marot and Caroline Pratt, Rita and Tom Benton, and Sally and Boardman Robinson, providing the right balance of society and solitude. Mumford reported that everyone walked, but he did note that Helen Marot had the only car among the group.[14]

Caroline and Helen spent the summers working on their professional pursuits, and swimming, driving, and visiting friends. They claimed to spend very quiet summers. The cottage was described as being a small house containing a comfortable large living room with chintz-covered couches and paneled walls.[15] It had a screen porch overlooking the water. Upstairs was a studio with a cot and a typewriter. Caroline and Helen valued the privacy afforded by the out of the way location of the cottage. As time went on they bemoaned the fact that the hill on which they were the first to build was becoming developed.

Benton and his wife in all likelihood had introduced the artist Jackson Pollock to the "two elderly women"[16] in the early 1930s. In the winter of 1934 when Jackson and his brother Sande were employed as school janitors, Caroline was 67 and Helen was 69. In the following years, Helen developed a close, almost maternal relationship with Jackson Pollock and he often visited their house on 12th Street—usually very late at night—in search of a sympathetic ear.

In the summer of 1937 when Caroline was 70 and Helen was 72, the interview mentioned at the beginning of this chapter took place. "What do you want with an interview with two old gals like us?" was the greeting the *Vineyard Gazette* reporter received. But they did agree to an interview. On the day of the meeting with the reporter, "Miss Pratt was reclining on a couch in the living room. 'I'm afraid I'm not up to talking much', she said, after she had explained briefly the aims of her educational work. 'See if you can get the rest of your interview from Miss Marot.' Then she called, 'I'm sending someone up to see you, Helen.'" Helen's information about Caroline's pioneering work at the City and Country School provided the majority of the text for the published interview.

Living Alone

Helen's sudden death on June 3, 1940, was a shock from which friends said that Caroline never completely recovered. It may have been responsible for a lengthy illness that was reported in the early months of 1941. In the summer of that year, she traveled to Kansas City to visit friends Tom and Rita Benton. Her brother, Henry, and his family came from their home in Oklahoma to visit her there. This is one of the only references to her family that was found. It seemed that after she completed her studies at Teachers College she began a life that didn't include family ties.

In later years, she shared her 12th Street apartment, just down the street from the school, with a huge cat. The apartment was cozy and comfortable with overstuffed furniture, pillows on the couches, and no television set, according to the memory of one of the teachers who took care of the cat when Caroline was away.

Principal Emerita

> *I have seen these teachers in whose hands the school remains,*
> *learning from the children as I learned myself,*
> *making sacrifices...to maintain...the standards*
> *to which we have all pledged ourselves.*[17]

After 31 years of intense involvement, Miss Pratt retired from active leadership of the City and Country School. She became Principal Emerita in June of 1945 at the age of 78. She stated emphatically in her autobiography that retiring was not an easy thing for her to do. She likened her feelings to the difficulty that a parent has to learn to accept the independence and decision making ability of an adolescent child. As a result, the last two years of her administration were difficult, because she was in the process of letting go of something that she had created and nurtured for 31 years. Replacing her at retirement was Miss Marion Carswell, who had previously served as principal of the Smith College Day School and had been a faculty member in the psychology department.

In November 1945, Caroline wrote to her longtime friend Fola LaFollette, "I'm out of the school pretty completely and very glad to be. I think they have the right kind of principal who will make every effort to carry on in the same way. On some things she is much better than I ever was. But she isn't creative and in this particular perhaps it is better."[18] Members of the school staff probably saw the picture a little differently, because several claimed that Pratt was quite involved with the school for some time after her retirement. While poor health prevented her from coming to the school very often, she "kept her finger on the pulse of the school" for two or three years after her retirement through frequent telephone calls.[19] It is also said that she would bribe City and Country students with candy when she met them on the street, in an effort to get them to tell her what was going on at school.

The situation had changed four years later. In a 1952 letter to Fola LaFollette, Leila Stott sent this report about Caroline, "She does not have much contact with the school any more and also does not seem to get the satisfaction I do myself out of seeing it running so well and so true to all her own standards."[20] It is possible that after Jean Murray became the principal in 1948, Caroline felt more able to "let go." Murray had been a teacher at City and Country, knew Caroline's philosophy and practice from years of experience, and was committed to carrying it forward. The two women who served briefly as principals after Caroline's retirement did not have the longterm connection with the school that Jean Murray had, and they may not have been able to communicate Caroline's principles with as much clarity as Murray could.

After Caroline's retirement, she returned to the writing of her autobiography, *I Learn from Children*. She credited Helen Marot with coming up with the title for the book, and the dedication reads, "to Helen Marot whose spirit still lives." She hadn't touched the manuscript for years until Leila Stott took responsibility to help Caroline complete it. The final version was prepared by Ruth Goode, a former parent and teacher at the school who spent an entire summer on Martha's Vineyard submitting changes to Caroline each week. A former teacher recalled that Caroline was delighted with the work of Goode and couldn't praise her enough. Caroline reportedly revealed that, "I couldn't say it. She said it just the way I wanted it to be said."

The collaborative effort was well received. A review in the *Martha's Vineyard Gazette* book review column, "The Vineyard

Bookshelf," on November 5, 1948, acknowledged that it was a "fascinatingly written book, full of a missionary personality." The reviewer related that the book describes how Miss Pratt's program was carried beyond the experimental stage "into the permanent sinew and blood of American education."

More than 40 reviews of *I Learn from Children* have been collected in the City and Country School archives, all containing praise for the book and recommendations for wider adoption of Miss Pratt's educational practices. Representative of the comments is this note to the publisher from Leo Huberman.

> Thank you for the copy of *I Learn from Children*. I have a direct personal interest in Caroline Pratt's book. I was one of the fortunate few who, for seven years, participated in her "adventure in progressive education." While we were all learning from children, we were also learning from her—the kind of simple everlasting truths that one gets only from truly great people. Much of that wisdom is captured in the pages of her book. That's why I hope that every parent—and every child—in the country will read it.[21]

Since its original publication in 1948, at a cost of $2.75, the book has been translated into at least ten languages and also reissued in a paperback version that is still in print.

In 1951, after living alone since Helen Marot's sudden death in 1940, Caroline hired a companion-housekeeper, Margaret Ryan. Ryan was thoughtful of Caroline and a gay companion, according to Leila Stott, who had assumed a protective role over Caroline in her later years. Sadly, Caroline's health failed considerably the last two years of her life. But her mind remained active. Stott claimed in a 1952 letter to LaFollette that while frail, "she is wonderful for her zest for life and interest in everything."[22] The following year, at the age of 86, Miss Pratt happily came out of retirement to observe the thirty-ninth anniversary of the City and Country school. She reiterated her firmly held position that it was an experimental school, and she made a point of stressing that the experiments were made *by* children and not *on* children.[23]

On June 6, 1954, less than a month after her eighty-seventh birthday, Caroline Pratt died of the consequences of a coronary thrombosis. Her obituary, almost a full column in the *New York Times*, was a final testament to the respect that she commanded in progressive educational circles. Leila Stott reported the details of

Caroline's death to Fola LaFollette in a letter written just five days later: "She had been relatively well up to the day before Easter when she was taken by what turned out to be a coronary thrombosis. Dr. wanted her to go at once to St. Luke's Hospital for oxygen treatment and she rallied from that attack but a second more serious one followed. The doctors thought she was dying then, and she herself prayed to go, but lingered on in semi-conscious condition until last Sunday morning. She did occasionally recognize some of us and seemed glad to know we were there, especially Margaret Ryan on whom she depended most of all and who was wonderful in her devotion. Roger Baldwin spoke at the simple funeral service for Caroline last Tuesday and really made us all feel as if Caroline herself was in our midst."[24]

A letter received by the Fayetteville historian, the month after Caroline's death, from an unidentified former resident of Fayetteville who was acquainted with Caroline, stated that before her death, "Caroline had a fairly comfortable winter and it was not until spring that she had a heart attack and finally spent the last two months of her life in St. Luke's hospital. She had a companion for the last two years who was very fond of her and of whom she was very fond, so she was happy and serene. Many people came to see her and she kept up an active interest in the school which she founded."[25]

Dorothy Van Doren, a former City and Country parent and widow of historian Mark Van Doren, had this comment on Pratt's funeral: "The originator and guiding spirit of the school our boys attended was not a religious woman, and at the funeral an old friend [Roger Baldwin] simply said a few things about her—that she loved children, that she had been fiercely true to the things she believed in, that children had liked and respected her." The service concluded with a former pupil, now grown up, playing something "touchingly familiar...a little Bach piece and part of a Mozart Sonata."[26]

Caroline Pratt was survived by her brother Henry Pratt then living in Kansas City, Missouri, and two nephews, Herbert of Tulsa Oklahoma, and Fayette of Norwood, Massachusetts. Her other siblings, Lizzie (Elizabeth) and John, had never married and predeceased her. In accordance with her will, her body was cremated. Her ashes were buried in the family plot in the Fayetteville Cemetery. The headstone bears the inscription,

Daughter
Caroline Pratt
May 13, 1867
June 6, 1954
I Learn From Children

Her nephew, Fayette D. Pratt, was named as her personal representative, but declined to serve, so Jean Murray, City and Country principal at the time and a close friend of Caroline's, made arrangements for the services and the disposition of her estate.

Her brother, Henry Pratt was the chief beneficiary of her will, but bequests were also made to Fred Taylor, Jack Humphreys, and Margaret Ryan, her housekeeper-companion. An abstract painting by Thomas Hart Benton that had hung in Caroline's home was given to Fola LaFollette. The Fayetteville Free Library received a bequest of two copies of *I Learn from Children*. No public records of other gifts have been found. It wasn't until 1966 that the City and Country School received the proceeds of the sale of her house on Martha's Vineyard. After being rented for a while, the house was sold in December 1965 for $24,000.

Clearly, Caroline Pratt's legacy is not the measure of her estate. Her work with children at the City and Country School and the influence that she has had on innumerable educators for nearly a century is the true measure of her contribution to the arts of teaching and learning.

Notes

1. *Martha's Vineyard Gazette*, Martha's Vineyard, MA, July 30, 1937.
2. Carlton, "Caroline Pratt: A Biography," 12. Information about Carlton's list of friends are all included in this chapter except for the actress, Katharine Cornell.
3. Chesler, *Margaret Sanger and the Birth Control Movement*, 106.
4. LC Manuscript Division, George Middleton Papers, Box 14.
5. Hirsch, "Caroline Pratt and the City and Country School: 1914-1945," 32, footnote 43.
6. Ibid., 37, 38.
7. Antler, *Lucy Sprague Mitchell: The Making of a Modern Woman*, 236.
8. Ibid., 241.
9. Eastman, *Love and Revelation: My Journey Through an Epoch*, 4.
10. Information from the Berkshire County Registry of Deeds, Pittsfield, Massachusetts, provided by Norton Owen, the current owner of the home.

11. *New York Times*, October 11, 1914. Information provided by Norton Owen.

12. Benton, *An Artist in America*, 4th edition, 344.

13. Ibid.

14. Lewis Mumford pp. 452-453.

15. *Martha's Vineyard Gazette*, July 30, 1937.

16. Neifeh and Smith, *Jackson Pollock An American Saga*.

17. LC, LaFollette Family Collection, Fola La Follette Section, Letter from Caroline Pratt to Fola LaFollette, November, 1945.

18. LC, LaFollette Family Collection. Fola La Follette Section. Miss Marion Carswell was appointed principal upon Caroline's retirement. She came from Smith College Day School and was a member of Smith's psychology department. Miss Charlotte Pinco, a City and Country School teacher, served as principal the following two years until Jean Wesson Murray, also a City and Country School teacher, began what would become a 30 year tenure as principal, almost equaling that of Miss Pratt.

19. Virginia Parker interview.

20. LC, LaFollette Family Collection, Fola LaFollette Section. Letter, January 27, 1952.

21. CCSA, Publications folder. Leo Huberman, best known as a socialist writer and editor, received a teaching degree from New York University and taught at the City and Country School for seven years, beginning in 1926.

22. LC, Follette Family Collection, Fola LaFollette Section letter, January 27, 1952.

23. Caroline Pratt Obituary, *New York Times*, June 7, 1954.

24. LC, LaFollette Family Collection, Fola LaFollette Section, letter July 11, 1954.

25. FFL, Fayetteville, NY, Letter dated July 21, 1954..

26. CCSA, Jean Murray Box.

CHAPTER TEN

The Legacy of Caroline Pratt and the City and Country School

*Schools that are laboratories in living and doing
offer education that is of more value to children
than adult-imposed book learning.*[1]

WHAT IS CAROLINE PRATT'S LEGACY for teachers and students? What value is added to our understandings of the teaching/learning process now that we have learned about her life and work? What meanings have readers constructed about this woman described in Chapter One as "complex"? Trying to articulate the responses to these questions was quite difficult until I realized I was trying to write about what I thought readers would see in Caroline's story. Clearly, I can only describe the consequences of Caroline Pratt's story for myself. Hopefully, my ideas may connect with and stimulate the thinking of readers.

Caroline inspired me the first time I read her autobiography in 1993. Early in my research I made notes about being impressed by her strong sense of personal identity and her courage not only to stand up for what she believed about education, but also to "do something about it" by establishing a school that would be an experimental environment for learning, an environment in which everyone was a learner. As I continued my research and learned about the personal dimension of her life as well as the professional dimension, my admiration increased. I admire her unapologetic pragmatism and her frank assessment of academe, even though I am a member of the academic community for which she had harsh words. Her perspective provides a welcome "reality check" about schooling because it comes from a practitioner whose ideas were based in her own experience.

The connections I made with her personal qualities validated my own professionalism. Knowing that she was part of the history of early childhood education gave me a sense of pride in my career. I would echo Stacie Goffin's assertion that she achieves satisfaction from the recognition that her efforts and those of her colleagues build upon those of her predecessors.[2] Teachers, especially teachers of young children, receive little public support for what they do. Finding historical connections with educators of Caroline Pratt's stature can validate a teacher's belief in what she or he does.

Her child-centered philosophy was another strong connection for me. In very direct language she stated the rationale for the importance of focusing the learning process on the child. This perspective demonstrates advocacy for children and advocacy for the best possible environment in which they can develop. City and Country School students were empowered in their learning because they had ownership of the curriculum. Today the emphasis on curriculum is on filling children with bits of information that someone (often someone far removed from the classroom) has decided is necessary for children to know. Since children are not able to advocate for themselves in the bureaucratic structure of schools, educators have a responsibility to stand up for children's rights to learn in a child-centered, constructivist environment. The practices that Caroline Pratt developed are a ready model. They have been shown to be effective in both public and private schools and with students who come from every point on the socioeconomic continuum.

In all of her work, she demonstrated a trust in children. She trusted their intelligence, their curiosity, their enthusiasm for learning. She prepared an environment in which children could direct their own learning and develop those important qualities. Too often we only give lip service to the idea that all children can learn. We focus on what children cannot do rather than what they can do. She reminds us of the potential of all children. Can the courage of her convictions inspire our advocacy for those we teach?

The idea that schooling should prepare students to engage in improving our democratic society is an important progressive education ideal that the City and Country School followed. A sense of community was built at the school, and all of the children had roles to play to make the community work well. Children were not told about democracy, they lived it and critiqued it. This legacy of Caroline Pratt's is also one to which we must attend. How can we create a democratic environment in our classrooms that will prepare children to participate in and strengthen the democracy in which we live?

Implications for Educational Policy

Caroline Pratt is part of a long tradition of educators who put children and their activity at the center of the curriculum. Comenius, Pestalozzi, Rousseau, Dewey, Piaget, and Vygotsky are also exponents of that tradition.[3] Marietta Johnson, Margaret Naumberg, Helen Parkhurst and Elsie Ripley Clapp, contemporaries of Miss Pratt, were also school-founders who were part of this child-centered tradition.[4] Sadly, a conservative political climate in the United States is endangering this child-centered tradition. Schooling is fast becoming a mechanical process in which student test scores define their "learning." Federal education programs, such as No Child Left Behind, that equate children's learning to scores on such "high stakes" testing fail to take into consideration critical aspects of the learning process such as Caroline Pratt emphasized at the City and Country School. The role of direct experience and play, the value of the arts, the benefit of curriculum integration to student learning, a focus on inquiry and critical thinking, and the power of collaboration were central to her program. She taught the whole child and she assessed the whole child. Narrative reports that documented children's participation in play activities, practical activities, skills or techniques, and enrichment of experience (the curricular categories Miss Pratt developed) provided a holistic and authentic picture of children's learning.

School reform, a common phrase of education policy discourse, takes on a new perspective in light of Caroline Pratt's work. She saw education as a transformative process. The transformation sprang from an independently educated individual who could think and make decisions for himself or herself. In contrast, the highly touted school reforms tend to be superficial structural events (akin to rearranging the deck chairs on the *Titanic*) that do not get to the heart of the needs that schools have.

In addition to the relevance that Caroline Pratt's ideas have to an examination of educational policy, her views on the role of teachers provide a perspective on current thinking about teachers. Each age group at the City and Country School had a social studies based curriculum. However, it was up to the teacher to enact that curriculum based on the questions/interests raised by the students. For the most part, Miss Pratt gave teachers a free hand to do this. She wanted her teachers to trust the students' ability to be active in constructing their knowledge, and she encouraged teachers to take a back seat in this process until students needed additional guidance. She saw teaching as an art. Unfortunately, when accountability for learning is only considered in terms of a numerical score on a test, teachers don't see themselves able to foster student leadership in determining how the curriculum will be enacted. Individual differences and interests in students and classes cannot be accommodated, because a teacher's time is given over to teaching to tests. Teaching is no longer an art. It is a mechanical process.

Unit Blocks

The Unit Blocks Caroline Pratt designed and constructed in 1913 for her first school are an enduring material legacy to early childhood education. Unfortunately, because the Unit Blocks do not bear her name, the legacy is an invisible one, a situation that I hope this book will help to remedy. To many educators and parents, blocks are the most valuable learning tools of early childhood and the Unit Blocks are the type favored by many early childhood practitioners. While there are many block varieties found in today's classrooms, Provenzo and Brett's observation about Unit Blocks, made in 1983, is still valid: "It is the standard block system used in most nursery schools today."[5] Along with Friedrich Froebel, they consider Pratt to be "the single person most responsible for introducing block building...into the curriculum of the schools...."[6] The importance Provenzo and Brett placed on Caroline Pratt's blocks is demonstrated by the fact that they included a chapter written by Harriet Johnson in 1933 in their book, *The Complete Block Book*. Johnson, an early collaborator of Miss Pratt, studied the use of Unit Blocks by children in the nursery school she directed. Children "graduated" from her school to the City and Country School. In her chapter, "The Art of Block Building," she described and illustrated the development of children's patterns of play with blocks as they reproduced their experiences.

Progressive or Feminist?

Caroline Pratt was a member of the progressive education movement, and the City and Country School she directed educated students in a thoroughly progressive tradition. Without denying her progressive practice, she refused to be placed in any ideological box and resisted requests to codify her ideas. To paraphrase Heterodoxy member Marie Jenney Howe,[7] Miss Pratt was an example of a practical liver of her own feminist theory. It is undoubtedly the case that she never articulated a feminist theory for herself. She probably would have protested that she was, to use a phrase that she applied to a different situation in her life, "too busy learning from children" to take time to reflect on her own personal development. But the way in which she lived her life, so different from the norm for women of the beginning of the twentieth century, embodied feminist ideals.

Miss Pratt actively sought a career in contrast to other young women of her time who waited at home for marriage. She sought out new experiences in every new place in which she found herself and wasn't constrained by "proper behavior" for women. She rejected the female mentality of service and self-sacrifice on behalf of men. She chose her own path in life, definitely at variance with many others. She valued freedom in her own life and in the education of her students.

Caroline Pratt drew strength and inspiration from both the expressionist progressives and the radical feminists of Greenwich Village. The woman she was and the school she shaped with such passion and energy for over 30 years are products of both of these influences. Our understanding of Caroline Pratt and her educational practice is richer because of both of these influences. By using a feminist perspective to understand her work we make sure that we celebrate the power of this perspective in understanding the educational process. Jennifer Wolfe, in *Learning from the Past*, advocates that we "reclaim the learnings and wisdom" of the "women who have been overlooked in the mainstream accounts and text of early childhood." "These were women full of passion, energy, and determination, deeply involved in educational reform."[8]

Miss Pratt's Challenge

Her own words, included in one of her early publications, remain an eloquent plea and reflect a confidence in the teachers who are yet to take their places in classrooms.

> It is hoped that our procedure will also fall into the hands of imaginative teachers to whom it will give courage to regard the fundamental principles of education, and to work out a new and perhaps better technique, and certainly one related to their own environment.[9]

A Final Tribute

The City and Country School has been able to survive for more than 90 years in part because of the strength of Miss Pratt's educational convictions about the value of play and direct experience in the learning process. Her convictions were based on observation of children, which shaped the curriculum she devised. Her unflagging faith in the ability of children to control their own learning has stood the test of time because it is based on the lived experience of children, not on abstractions of children, nor on disconnected elements in children's environments, but on a holistic perspective of children. We need to be reminded of the holistic way in which children learn. We need to read about ways in which children are active in the learning process.

The following tribute to Caroline Pratt was published in the *New York Times*, shortly after she died. It was written by Charles A. Reich, a graduate of City and Country School and an attorney, writer, and social critic. It is a fitting conclusion to this discussion of her legacy to education.

> Our schools owe a great debt to Caroline Pratt, whose long and creative life ended this week. She knew that learning can be an exciting adventure. She was able to sharpen, not blunt, the natural intellectual curiosity of children. They went eagerly to her City and Country School. Many of the methods of teaching she pioneered came to be accepted within her lifetime and, wherever they were schooldays are happier and more rewarding.[10]

I could find no better expression of the power of Caroline Pratt's ideas.

Notes

1. CP, "Learning by Experience," *Child Study*, 71.
2. Goffin, "We Are Not Champions of a Newly Discovered Cause: Remembering the Heroines of Early Childhood Education" *Young Children*.
3. John Amos Comenius (1592-1670), Jean-Jacques Rousseau (1712-1778), Johann Heinrich Pestalozzi (1746-1827), John Dewey (1859-1952), Jean Piaget (1896-1980), and Lev Vygotsky (1896-1934) are educational leaders who espoused what is generally referred to as a constructivist way of learning. This list is selective, however, and others are also part of this tradition.
4. Biographies of these and other progressive educators can be found in Sadovnik and Semel, *Founding Mothers and Others: Women Educational Leaders in the Progressive Era.*
5. Provenzo and Brett, *The Complete Block Book*, 31.
6. Ibid., 27.
7. Wittenstein, "The Heterodoxy Club and American Feminism, 1912-1930."
8. Wolfe, *Learning from the Past*, 395.
9. CP, *Experimental Practice in the City and Country School*, 2.
10. Charles A. Reich, Letter to the Editor, *New York Times*, June 7, 1954.

Methodology Notes

A biography, no matter how thoroughly researched, is always a partial telling of a story. The partial nature of the telling is related to many elements that combine in a myriad of patterns to define the story. I have selected four elements to consider in the preparation of Caroline Pratt's biography. First, the quantity of material available shapes the completeness and the detail of the story that can be told. For example, the biography of an individual who was an active correspondent with family and friends and colleagues can provide a rich source of personal information that brings the chronology to life. Professional publications that have been preserved and records of professional organizations help the biographer reconstruct the development of career paths.

Second, the nature of available resources is also a factor in a biography's construction. Primary sources such as personal diaries, business correspondence, professional writing, and interviews of recollections from friends and family, if available, can provide direct information to the biographer. Photographs and artifacts (such as a family Bible) can be studied for additional information. Secondary sources, writings about the writings of the subject of the biography, provide information as well, but must be carefully considered because they add a layer of interpretation as well.

A third element are the decisions made by the writer as to what to include and what not to include to shape the story. Some of these decisions are consciously made. Every biographer faces ethical dilemmas about whether or not to make public information about the subject that he or she considers could be negatively interpreted by the reader or that doesn't seem to be consistent with the persona that is being constructed in the biography. Other choices are unconsciously determined by the author's personal construction of reality, the lens through which he or she understands the world.

A final consideration in the telling of a story is the role of the reader. What story will the reader construct? The reader, just as the writer, applies lenses to his or her understanding of the events described. What parts of the account are ignored; what parts are altered to fit the worldview of the reader?

APPENDIX B

Publications of Caroline Pratt

1903

Marot, Helen. "Report of an investigation made in Philadelphia," (Philadelphia: Philadelphia Branch of the Consumers' League), with Caroline Pratt.

1911

"Toys: A Usurped Educational Field." *The Survey, A Journal of Constructive Philanthropy*, 26 (The Charitable Organization of the City of New York), 893-95.

1913

"Tools vs Rules," *The American Teacher*, September, 98-101.

1914

"The Real Joy in Toys," *Parents and Their Problems: Child Welfare in Home, School, Church, and State*, Vol. 4 Mary Harmon Weeks, ed. (Washington D.C.: The National Congress Mothers and Parent-Teacher Associations), 114-123.

1917

The Play School: An Experiment in Education (New York: Bureau of Educational Experiments).

1919

"Experimental Schools," *The Dial*, 66, April 19, 413-415.

1921

Forward to the *Here and Now Story Book: Two to Seven Year Olds*, by Lucy Sprague Mitchell (New York: E. P. Dutton), ix-xii.

"Introduction" to *City and Country Record of Group VI*, by Leila Stott, (New York: City and Country School), 7-8.

1924
Experimental Practice in the City and Country School. (New York: E.P. Dutton & Co.), with Lula E. Wright.

1925
"Originality in Children," Book review of *The Psychology of the Preschool Child* by Bird T. Baldwin and Lorle I. Stecher. *The Nation*, 121:3147, 493 (November 28).

"Collective Formulations in Curriculum," *Progressive Education*, 11:4, 231-235.

1926
Before Books (New York: Adelphi Co.), with Jessie Stanton.

"Curriculum Making in the City and Country School," *26ᵗʰ Yearbook of the National Society for the Study of Education.* Bloomington, IN, pp. 327-331.

1927
"Making Environment Meaningful," *Progressive Education*, 4:1 105-108.

1929
"Children in Their Neighborhoods," *Child Study*, 6:5, 110-112.

1930
"Two Basic Principles of Education," *New Republic*, July 2, 172-176.

1931
"Growing Up and Dramatics," *Progressive Education*, 8:1, 7-9.

1932
"Growing Up and Dramatics," in *Creative Expression*, G. Hartman and Ann Shumaker, eds. (New York: John Day Co, 1931), 262-265.

1933
"Learning by Experience," *Child Study*, 11:3, 69-71.

1934
"As to Indoctrination," *Progressive Education*, Jan-Feb, 106-119.

1935
"Social Experiences—Not Social Studies," *Educational Method* 15:2, (National Education Association), 101-104.

1936
"Imagination and Literature," *Progressive Education*, 13:8, 617-620.

"Recording Mental Health and Treatment," *Progressive Education*, 13: 1, 27-31.

1937
Foreword to *The Place of Reading and Social Science in a Job-Centered School*, by Bertha Delanty and Sybil May (New York: 69 Bank Street), 1-3.

1938
"Animal, or Vegetable?" *New York Teacher*, 3:8 (The Teachers Union Local 5 AFT), May, 12-13.

1940
"Coming of Age in America: Michael," *Progressive Education* 17:8, 553-557.

1948
I Learn from Children: An Adventure in Progressive Education (New York: Simon and Schuster).

1949
I Learn from Children (excerpts from the book) *Omnibook—The Book Magazine*, 11:2, 29-35. January.

1970
I Learn from Children (New York: Harper & Row).

1973
[1917} Experimental Schools Revisited (Bulletin #3), The Play School: An Experiment in Education, with Lucille Deming, edited with an introduction by Charlotte Winsor (New York: Agathon Press).

APPENDIX C

Unit Blocks

This illustration is from the files of the City and Country School archives.

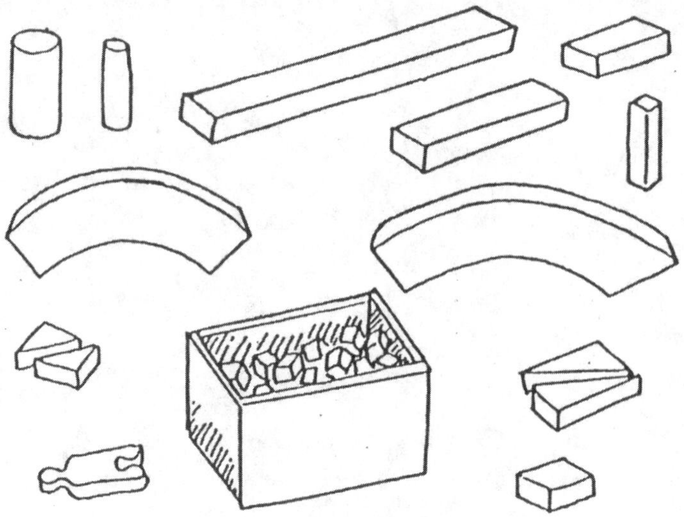

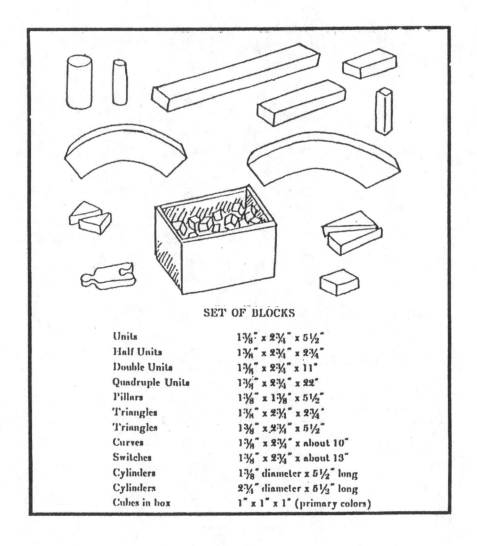

SET OF BLOCKS

Units	1⅜" x 2¾" x 5½"
Half Units	1⅜" x 2¾" x 2¾"
Double Units	1⅜" x 2¾" x 11"
Quadruple Units	1⅜" x 2¾" x 22"
Pillars	1⅜" x 1⅜" x 5½"
Triangles	1⅜" x 2¾" x 2¾"
Triangles	1⅜" x 2¾" x 5½"
Curves	1⅜" x 2¾" x about 10"
Switches	1⅜" x 2¾" x about 13"
Cylinders	1⅜" diameter x 5½" long
Cylinders	2¾" diameter x 5½" long
Cubes in box	1" x 1" x 1" (primary colors)

Bibliography

Adler, Margot. *The Heretic Heart*. Boston: Beacon Press, 1997.

Antler, Joyce. "Feminism as life process: The life and career of Lucy Sprague Mitchell." *Feminist Studies* 7 (1981): 134-157.

————. *Lucy Sprague Mitchell: The Making of a Modern Woman*. New Haven, CT: Yale University Press, 1987.

Asher, Carol, Louise DeSalvo, and Sara Ruddick. *Between Women*. Boston: Beacon Press, 1984.

Beatty, Barbara. *Preschool Education in America*. New Haven, CT: Yale University Press, 1995.

Beck, Robert. "American Progressive Education 1875-1930," Ph.D. diss., New Haven, CT, Yale University, 1942/1965: 129-137.

————. "Progressive Education and American Progressivism: Caroline Pratt," *Teachers College Record 60*, no 3 (1958): 129-137.

Benton, Thomas Hart. *An Artist in America*, 4th edition, Columbia, MO: University of Missouri Press, 1983.

Bode, Boyd. *Progressive Education at the Crossroads*. New York: Newson & Co., 1938.

Brosterman, Norman. *Inventing Kindergarten*. New York: Harry V. Adams, 1997.

Caplan, Frank, and Theresa Caplan. *The Power of Play*. New York: Anchor Press, 1973.

Carlton, Patricia. "Caroline Pratt: A Biography." Ph.D. diss. New York: Teachers College, Columbia University, 1986.

Chesler, Ellen. *Margaret Sanger and the Birth Control Movement in America*. New York: Simon and Shuster, 1992.

City and Country School Bulletin Board, April 1936. CCSA.

City and Country School Catalogue, 1921-1922. Author. CCSA.

City and Country School, Inc., The. Unpublished manuscript, nd. CCSA.

Conway, Jill Kerr. *When Memory Speaks*. New York: Vintage, 1998.

Cott, Nancy. *The Grounding of Modern Feminism*. New Haven, CT: Yale University Press, 1987.

Cremin, Lawrence. *The Transformation of the School: Progressivism in American Education, 1876-1957*. New York: Alfred Knopf, 1961.

Cremin, Lawrence, David A. Shannon, and Mary Evelyn Townsend. *History of Teachers College Columbia University*. New York: Columbia University Press, 1954.

Crocco, Margaret Smith, Petra Munro, and Kathleen Weiler. *Pedagogies of Resistance: Women Educator Activists, 1880-1960*. New York: Teachers College Press, 1999.

Delahanty, Bernice, and Sybil May. "The Place of Reading and Social Science in a Job-centered School," Bank Street Bulletin, 3:6, March, 1937: 3-12.

De Lima, Agnes. *Our Enemy the Child*. New York: New Republic, 1926.

Dewey, John. *The School and Society*. Chicago: University of Chicago Press, 1899.

Dewey, John, and Evelyn Dewey. *Schools of Tomorrow*. New York: E.P. Dutton, 1915.

Eastman, Max. *Love and Revelation: My Journey Through an Epoch*. New York: Random House, 1964.

Encyclopedia Britanica 2006. *Encyclopedia Brittanica Premium Service*. 26 Jan. 2006. http://www.britanica.com/eb/article?tocld-9070834.

Franklin, Adele, and Agnes E. Benedict. *Play Centers for School Children*. New York: William Morrow, 1943.

Goffin, Stacie. "We Are Not Champions of a Newly Discovered Cause: Remembering the Heroines of Early Childhood Education." *Young Children*, 47 (November, 1991): 62-64.

Graham, Patricia Albjerg. *Progressive Education: From Arcady to Academe*. New York: Teachers College Press, 1967.

Hale, Beatrice Forbes-Robertson. *What Women Want*. New York: Frederick A. Stokes, 1914.

Hansen, Mary D. "About the Caroline Pratt Unit Blocks," The City and Country School, upublished pamphlet, 1990.

Hauser, Mary. "Caroline Pratt and the City and Country School," in *Founding Mothers and Others: Women Educational Leaders During the Progressive Era*, edited by Alan Sadovnik and Susan Semel, 61-76. New York: Palgrave, 2002.

Henderson, Charles Hanford. *Education and the Larger Life*. New York: Houghton, Mifflin and Co., 1902.

Hervey, Walter L. "Historical Sketch of Teachers College from Its Foundation to 1897." *Teachers College Record 1* (1900):12-35.

Hirsch, Maxine. "*Caroline Pratt and the City and Country School, 1914-1945.*" Ph.D. diss., Rutgers University, New Jersey, 1986.

Irwin, Elisabeth, and Louis Marks. *Fitting the School to the Child: An Experiment in Public Education*. New York: Macmillan, 1928.

James, Edward ed. *Notable American Women, Vol II*. Cambridge, MA: Radcliffe College, 1971.

Kilpatrick, William. "The Project Method," *Teachers College Record* 19 (1918).

Lascarides, V. Celia, and Blythe Hinitz. *History of Early Childhood Education*. New York: Falmer Press, 2000.

Levin, Robert A. "The Debate over Schooling," *Childhood Education*, Winter, 1991:

Marcus, Lloyd. "The Founding of American Private Progressive Schools 1912-1921," Harvard University senior thesis, 1948.

Marot, Helen. *Creative Impulse in Industry: A Proposition for Educators*. New York: E.P. Dutton, 1918.

———. "The Play School: An Experiment," *The New Republic* (November 6, 1915): 16-17.

Mitchell, Lucy Sprague. *Two Lives: The Story of Wesley Clair Mitchell and Myself*. New York: Simon and Schuster, 1953.

Mumford, Lewis. *Sketches from Life*. New York: Dial Press, 1982.

Naifeh, Steven, and Gregory White Smith. *Jackson Pollock: An American Saga*. New York: Clarkson Potter, Inc., 1989.

Palmieri, Patricia Ann. *In Adamless Eden*. New Haven, CT: Yale University Press, 1995.

Pratt, Caroline. "As to Indoctrination," *Progressive Education* (Jan-Feb 1934): 106-119.

———. "Collective Formulations in Curriculum," *Progressive Education* 11:4 (October, November, December, 1925): 231-235.

————. *Experimental Practice in the City and Country School*. New York: E.P. Dutton, 1924.

————. *I Learn from Children*. New York: Harper & Row, 1970.

————. "Jobs and How They Have Been Chosen," unpublished manuscript, CCSA.

————. "Learning by Experience," *Child Study*, 11, no 3 (December 1933): 69-71.

————. "Making Environment Meaningful," *Progressive Education* 4:1(1927): 105-108.

————. Foreword to "The Place of Reading and Social Science in a Job-centered School," New York: Bank Street Bulletin, 3:6. (March, 1937): 1-3.

————. "The Play School," Bulletin #3. New York: Bureau of Educational Experiments, 1917.

————. "Toys: A Usurped Educational Field," *Survey*: 26 (September 23, 1911): 893-895.

————. "Two Basic Principles of Education, *The New Republic*, July 2, 1930: 172-176.

Pratt, Caroline, and Jessie Stanton. *Before Books*. New York: Adelphi, 1926.

Provenzo, Eugene F., Jr., and Arlene Brett. *The Complete Block Book*. Syracuse NY: Syracuse University Press, 1983.

Rugg, Harold, and Ann Schumacher. *The Child-Centered School: An Appraisal of the New Education*. Yonkers-on-Hudson, New York: World Book Co., 1928.

Sadovnik, Alan, and Susan Semel, eds. *Founding Mothers and Others: Women Educational Leaders During the Progressive Era*. New York: Palgrave, 2002.

Schwarz, Judith. *Radical Feminists of Heterodoxy*. Norwich, VT: New Victoria Publishers, 1986.

Seller, Maxine. "G. Stanley Hall and Edward Thorndike on the Education of Women." *Educational Studies* 11:4, 1981: 365-374.

Semel, Susan. "Female Founders and the Progressive Paradox," In *Social Reconstruction through Education: The Philosophy, History and Curricula of a Radical Ideal*, Michael E. James, ed., 92-96. Norwood, New Jersey: Ablex, 1995.

Semel, Susan, and Alan Sadovnik, eds. *"Schools of Tomorrow," Schools of Today: What Happened to Progressive Education?* New York: Peter Lang, 1999.

Semel, Susan, and Alan Sadovnik. "Lessons from the Past: Individualism and Community in Three Progressive Schools." *Peabody Journal of Education*, 70 (Summer, 1995): 56-85.

Shapiro, Edna K., and Nancy Nager. "Remembering Schools: Recollections of Graduates of Early Progressive Schools." New York: CCSA unpublished manuscript, n.d.

Sochen, June. *Movers and Shakers, American Women Thinkers and Activists 1900-1970.* New York: Quadrangle, 1973.

Smith-Rosenberg, Carroll. *Disorderly Conduct: Visions of Gender in Victorian America.* New York: Knopf, 1985.

Stack, Sam F., Jr. *Elsie Ripley Clapp (1879-1965): Her Life and the Community School.* New York: Peter Lang, 2004.

Stott, Leila V. "Teachers in War Time." *Progressive Education* 21 (March, 1943).

Vineyard Gazette, various issues, Martha's Vineyard, MA.

Vygotsky, L.S. *Mind and Society.* Cambridge, MA: Harvard University Press, 1978.

Ware, Caroline. *Greenwich Village, 1920-1930.* Berkeley: University of California Press, 1963.

Weekly Recorder, various issues, Fayetteville, NY: FFL library microfiche.

Weiler, Kathleen. "Reflections on Writing a History of Women Teachers," *Harvard Educational Review* 67:4, 1997: 635-657.

Winsor, Charlotte. "Blocks as a Material for Learning through Play." In Elisabeth S. Hirsch, ed., *The Block Book, third edition*, 1-8. Washington, D.C.: National Association for the Education of Young Children, 1996.

Winsor, Charlotte, ed. *Experimental Schools Revisited: Bulletins of the Bureau of Educational Experiments*, Bulletin #3. New York: Agathon Press, 1973.

Wittenstein, Kate. "The Heterodoxy Club and American Feminism, 1912-1930," Ph.D. diss. Boston University,1989.

Wolfe, Jennifer. *Learning from the Past: Historical Voices in Early Childhood Education.* Mayerthorpe, Alberta, Canada: Piney Branch Press, 2000.

Zorach, William. *Art Is My Life: The Autobiography of William Zorach.* New York: World Publishing, 1967.

Index

THIS SERIES EXPLORES THE HISTORY OF SCHOOLS AND SCHOOLING in the United States and other countries. Books in this series examine the historical development of schools and educational processes, with special emphasis on issues of educational policy, curriculum and pedagogy, as well as issues relating to race, class, gender, and ethnicity. Special emphasis will be placed on the lessons to be learned from the past for contemporary educational reform and policy. Although the series will publish books related to education in the broadest societal and cultural context, it especially seeks books on the history of specific schools and on the lives of educational leaders and school founders.

For additional information about this series or for the submission of manuscripts, please contact the general editors:

Alan R. Sadovnik   Susan F. Semel
Rutgers University-Newark   The City College of New York, CUNY
Education Dept.   138th Street and Convent Avenue
155 Conklin Hall   NAC 5/208
175 University Avenue   New York, NY 10031
Newark, NJ 07102

To order other books in this series, please contact our Customer Service Department:

800-770-LANG (within the U.S.)
212-647-7706 (outside the U.S.)
212-647-7707 FAX

Or browse online by series at:

www.peterlang.com